Contents

Introduction

I write this book and dedicate it to all the old boys who ran at the match all of those years ago. Let's face it a lot of us did it, and a lot of us people don't like to admit it, and keep stum about it. Us LFC fans should be the ones who most shouldn't admit it. But, why deny the truth, it happened and it developed from the violent culture which originated from the 1970s. I have tried to include some seeds of how these violent streaks emerged from the 70s. I always remember the silly chant a. g. agr. Agro. AGGRO, this was accepted and being hard, or even just acting hard and was a defence mechanism to get by in scary places at scary times. Even during the daily playground fight's nobody was really safe from physical and mental abuse. But I did attend one of Britain's worst performing schools, so maybe we got the worst of it. The whole Huyton's schools have now been abandoned by the local kids who nearly all attend schools in the relatively safe city of Liverpool instead of the tough town of Huyton.

Surviving in the council estates made us ripe to be top notch hooligans. The more working class we were, the more we were prone to be involved. During the bleak economic climate there was a feeling of governmental abandonment and hate towards scousers that seemed to exuberate the situation and stir up the stew of violence that was about to hit our country. Angry young men with a good reason to be angry is a very dangerous mix.

I do believe there was people from all walks of life who were mixed up in this all for the buzz, but we were the ones who made it all happen and we were the core of the idea. We had genuine anger and took it out on all who tried to steal our thunder.

There was a great feeling of camaraderie that we couldn't find anywhere else. The situation meant that there was not a lot of jobs out there and it was the only place to meet new people, make friends and do something together. It was so bleak that I never really got my first job until I was 22, thanks Maggie for fucking up our chances, trying to decline our city, forgetting about the counties future generation and generally pissing on the working class. I still sound angry, I suppose it never leaves you, it makes you who you are, an x-hooligan with nostalgic thoughts of happy days running through the danger with the boys and feeling like a unit taking on the world for your team's pride.

Don't get me wrong though, it's not all about scousers. It's about the working class lads and girls who grew up in that era. Manchester, Birmingham, London, Newcastle, Sheffield, Nottingham, Bristol, Glasgow and Cardiff we were all the same fighting for our team and for our generation, letting off steam and releasing our anger. Some people say it had no point, it was just mindless thuggery, but I disagree, it was our generation protesting against our oppression by the powers-that-be.

So I must apologise if my use of diction is not what it should be and vocabulary is somewhat limited. I did get my English GCSE but I was 47 at the time. I also got a degree in Education to understand where my teachers went wrong in our era, but all I really learned when looking back is 90 percent of them couldn't give a shit about us. It's a wonder how our generation turned out so well, it was probably something to do with our good family values and well principled, old fashioned upbringing by our parents who went through the second world war. Err... good luck this generation all you've got is social media and reality TV. Give me some wits a field and a football and I'll show you another world completely.

1

QPR away

The lads wanted to go to every ground in the first division that included more obscure ones like QPR.

Rod and Remo were loitering in the Las Vegas arcade waiting for the boys to arrive. Remo had a clicker which was a gas cooker lighter. He was constantly looking for the staff to walk away then madly clicking at the coin slot. Eventually he would hit lucky and get 99 credits which he usually bagged about six quid from. Rod and Remo legged it over the road, Remo's tracksuit bottoms were jingling with the change. They both shot up the concourse onto the Station roof again. Gio, John, Fergo, Boiler, Jaffa, Yoggie and Longy were waiting for them.
"Any change for a cup a' tea Remo".
The lads laughed and Rod lit up another spliff. "I've got some speed today lads, anyone fancy trying it".
Gio declined as his LSD trip went the wrong way one day. Rod, John and Remo popped one each.
"How we getting on the train today lads, the word is they've beefed security up since we last got through the turnstiles."
Yoggie perked up and said he had a new way. What he explained was his mate was in the army and had an extra strong rope. All they had to do was bunk into the Postal headquarters, and lower each other down, only about 30 foot. As they put the plan into action a dog tried to chase them but was restrained by a big lead and Porker who was the son of a copper wasn't happy hanging 30 foot up and not good at supporting his own weight. He managed to slip 25 foot but then grabbed onto the rope for dear life. His palms were all burnt, but give the lad credit he carried on with the trip. The lads were all ribbing him and saying he has a bad habit and that he should get a bird instead, as this was the only cure to burnt palms.
Gio and Remo ended up kicking each other and one of Remo's trabs fell off during his descent. Now Remo was not overly fond of this pair, but he didn't want them ran over. The early morning London train had just departed from

platform 9 and he scrambled across the tracks to rescue his right trainer, from almost total destruction.

As they all reached the tracks they legged it across about 7 rails, they looked like modern-day refugee's trying to enter another country, but it was the match which was their passion.

A train was leaving and honked its powerful horns. The lads all gave the driver 'V' signs and Remo was even doing some tightrope walking on the same track in front of the train, happy that he now had two shoes. The crew all opened multiple doors and entered one carriage to London. They also had a fake ticket from the last trip. The date was changed and it was photocopied so they didn't have to hide from the conductor.

A few verses of Liverpool win away were sung, then Porky is a wanker.

Then the first stop was Runcorn were a few Chester City fans got on. They were all scarfer's as was half the nation, before scally culture took hold. Five of the lads went over to talk to them. "Where are you from lads"? Rod asked. "Liverpool" was the reply. Where about "Chester" they replied. "Fuck, Chester's not in Liverpool." The scousers were laughing their balls off. One of the Chester lads said they had a nasty rivalry with Wrexam. He explained that there was an ancient thing going on about it. When Wales and England had wars in the dark ages, that hatred had transferred to the modern day. "Them Welsh are fucking mental, they hate us with a passion. It's a nation thing. They are as bad as the Jocks. English bastards this, English bastards that, they think we have all the benefits, we said they got all the sheep." The lads had a good talk to Chester and said next time they played Wrexham that they would give them a hand.

As the train pulled into Euston there was no other fans about so the lads jumped straight over the turnstiles onto the blue line to Oxford Circus, then it would be the red line towards Latin road and Wood Lane. As they got off at Oxford Circus they saw a big mob on the other side of the platform. Then the chant went up "Miiiiiiilllllllllllwwwwwaaaaaaaaaallllll". The Road End boys responded as they didn't feel scared "The Road End, the Road End.", "We hate cockneys and we hate cockneys". Some nutter tried to cross the track but as he tried to get on the scousers platform he got kicked three times in the stomach. There was an electric central line and he managed to skip over it as he fell, which was just as well, or he would have been a Kentucky fried cockney. Then the charge began up through the connecting tube. "Fucking Millwall, what a reputation we'll have if we do these."Fergo shouted "Let's do them" It was like that in the 80's if you did the top firm, even if it was a small element of them then you shouted about it. As the two crews met you could notice who was who as Millwall still had about 70% boot boys and Liverpool were all well and truly casual hardcore. Jaffa was the first to get a kick in, some cockney held his stomach like he couldn't hold in last night's curry. Jaffa had his Liverpool hat on again, as he was still a big fan of the football, and that's when Millwall knew they had met the scousers. Some Millwall seemed to stand back as they realised these could be the famous Stanley boys. Liverpool surged into them as they hesitated. Everyone's faces were contorted with violence and anger towards their cockney tormentors. Anger towards the South and London was hardwired into their minds, as they did seem to have all the jobs and wealth down there, but nothing changes much over time. The scousers steamed through the doorway, that's when they got a surprise. The boys who had legged it were just the juniors from their crew, behind them you could see the hardcore men. The trouble being that the men could not get past the boys who were by this time getting mullered. Five Millwall were down on the floor. The Road End boys numbered only thirty but this was one narrow corridor. Normal people screamed and scarpered in every direction. Some woman with a pram tried to get in but Remo helped her back out of the corridor. John and Gio grabbed some plastic light holder and ragged it from the ceiling about to throw it at Millwall, but as Gio yanked it, then it must have caused a short and the whole corridor went dark. The door seemed to be jammed and the scousers simply had to fight for it, or be mullered by the big lads at the back. But they still couldn't get past the juniors who were still fighting back trying to make a name for themselves. But it was simply too dark and Remo ended up punching some of his own, Gio hit Rod and knocked him down. "This is fucking stupid, we don't know who were fighting with". The Millwall men shouted "mooooove" towards their junior crew, who tried their best to get up, but were still getting twatted by the scousers. Rod and John managed to force the door open and the scousers piled out and back onto the platform, time for a retreat as they realised how outnumbered they were again. They threw three bins at the juniors and two lads held the door shut with a chair as the scousers piled onto any train, not even knowing what line it was. It did happen to be the right train but the scousers had got a taste for chaos now and decided to get off at the next station. They went past Green Park and it stopped at London Victoria. This seemed to serve the South coast cities and this is where they clashed with the famous 657 crew. Now Gio had gone down to Portsmouth in 1980 and knew what to expect. The city was served by a big Docks community and these lads were as working class as the scouser's themselves. It seems that every decent sized city has some working class areas, and the outlook on life was very much the same wherever you went. There was about 25 of them and with 30 scousers this would be a nice even fight. Portsmouth were in the second division and were playing Watford this day, they just didn't expect a ruck with scousers but it was always welcome. Victoria was a big station with a lot of people in it, so it would cause panic and big problems this time of day.

Rod looked up and had an idea "Southampton, Southampton" he shouted. All the boys looked around that's when the pompey charged, they had been wound up by one little chant, that's all it took. Three lads at the front had taken the innards out of some bins and one hit Rod on the head. It fucking bounced like an Ian Rush header and hit another lad. It just riled up Rod who lashed out at them. This was a great ruck as everybody knew it was even numbers, so who ever won knew that it was a fair fight. Dockers kids onto dockers kids, this was the life. John got an uppercut into some lads face a big cut opened on his face and he fell back. Gio got another bin innards smashed into his face and his nose exploded. This didn't hold Gio back though and he carried on wind-milling with his fists, blinded by the blood he just lashed out. This looked like it was going to be a long and sustained battle. They pulled off a little, then they steamed back in with the shout of "657". The road end boys, then pulled back a little and there was a standoff. The sound of police whistles was probably going to put a stop to this, but not just yet it was too intense. It was Remo and Fergo who started the surge back to Pompey with a cry of "Liverpool" and a couple of plastic chairs got lobbed. The battle intensified and there were some big lads in the Pompey crew who were just not moving. The road end boys were used to other crews moving, but these and Millwall were really hard-core fighters, this was getting a little bit scary. That's when the bizzies arrived with dogs and truncheons. They were on 'auto-smash' and steamed into both sets of fans.

Nobody wanted to get arrested so the two crews scarpered in different directions. The scousers left the station and decided to pursue some 'shop-time' to top up their gear. Gio in particular wanted a new top as his blue and white benneton top was ruined with the claret paint that had leaked from his snoz. "Fuckin 'ell Rob this is a great day we're having. What you trying for, to replace the top lad ?" Gio looked around and then at his top. "I've always wanted a navy blue lacoste t-shirt, I reckon that's next. Oh, and a Fila NB top, let's see what we can find down here." The whole crew stormed through some sort of high street, they didn't even know what it was called. Their plan was to acquire some stuff then find another subway station to get to QPR's Loftus Road station. Nobody had done their research but Rod had earlier kicked a tourist machine that held maps, loads had leaked out. The lads started to leg it down the street, they were kicking over everything in their way including a burger stand. Some old hot dog man got brown sauce squirted all over his head, it was Johns trick again. The lads then saw a newspaper stand and booted over all the red tops as they were usually full of shit. Remo grabbed a load of porno mags and gave them out. That's when they saw the golfing shop, it was ripe for picking. The roar went up and the traffic stopped as they all charged over the road. The lads shouted abuse and gave nasty hand signals at the drivers who tried to carry on and stormed into the shop. The shopkeepers looked shocked as this shop usually attracted middle aged men and middle class clientele. There was three people in the shop and only 4 shop assistants. The men all had bright looking pastel jumpers on. The mob were intent on robbery. Rod shouted "We want it, we want it all". Remo and Fergo started laughing at him as he definitely looked like he was on something. The shop keepers looked stunned but one tried to put his hands around a zig full of lacoste t-shirts, Gio was having none of it and booked at the zig. Loads of t-shirts flew off and the shop keeper retreated. One shopkeeper shouted "We've rung the police". Remo looked up and shoted "Well done, but we'll be well gone by the time they get here, we're fucking timing experts." Multiple zigs went down and the middle aged pricks ran out of the shop, surprisingly one of them grabbed a few jumpers before he left. It just shows that a bit of anarchy and everybody will join in, no matter what your usual behaviour is. John now had a lovely tacchinni top on in dark purple with red stripes, he also had two pairs of tacchinni track suit bottoms on. "Fuckin 'ell

John your gonna have some sweaty arse running around the smoke." The elasticised bottoms were both different sizes so he just pulled the rope pull tightest it could go. The crew knew they had a finite time to rob then they had to get out of there fast, especially as they had already been face to face with the pigs today. The sirens were already in the distance when the colourful pirates stormed back out of the shop and ran straight into the nearest subway station called Slone Square. As they ran past a busker, Gio looked at him and shouted "You scruffy cockney, get that washed and become a casual lad". Gio threw his blood splattered Fila t-shirt at him, then started wild laughter. "Do your witch laugh", John said to Gio. Gio did a high pitched laugh that reverberated around the subway walls, it was an exact copy of what the wicked witch did in The wizard of Oz and it did make everybody look around in horror and wait for green smoke to appear from somewhere. Rod stopped and everybody looked around as he looked like a Japanese tourist with his concertina map hanging down, he was looking for which train they should get. He thought it was a fucking family outing. Green track to Hammersmith, then change for wood lane or Hammersmith.

"Alright fuckin' blakey. I wouldn't mind getting hammered in a place called Hammersmith, but we've got too much gear. Shepard's bush sounds like a farmers daughter's promise, but same story, we've got too much to lose." Fergo looked on "Straight to Wood lane then and the Queens Park Rangers, and let's see if we can find Boo boo bear with his mates."

The boys started singing their anthem "We're the barmy, Annie Road Army". The passengers were very diverse and different, but the boys didn't believe in picking on the general public. It was an un written law to leave the people alone, we would let them know who we were. We let them know that we are the best. Some Asian man had been having palpitations and a panic attack. One of the lads went over and reassured him that we were just messing about and never picked on nobody because of his colour or creed, we just wanted our casual rivals.

As the boys got off their train at Hammersmith, there was another gang waiting. They were boot boys, and some of them were really old.

Remo was really riled up "Fucking hell it's the Leeds Long booted legends, fuckin boot boys, lets 'av them." There was about twenty of them and they were

game. Some of them even had their striped yellow and white scarves on they were really old school. But them boots really were effective. Some twat even had a steel top bit on his spoonies. Never-the-less it was time to steam in or be steamed. Remo did one of this high kick karate things and hit some poor sod straight in the mush. This lad went down like a German Messerschmitt in 44. But there was this big lad, he must have been six foot four and about aged 30. Nobody knew where he came from but it could have been Fred Flintstone by the size of his arms. He was swinging them around and bashing scouser's all over the show. It was Gio's turn to test himself on a caveman. Gio was six foot one and quite large in stature but still only 17 and growing. He grabbed this feller by his tree trunk arm and dug his nails in like a girl. The man swivelled his trunk around to face Gio square in the face, his eyes were wild with violent madness. But his eyes were rimmed with glasses with the thickest lenses Gio had ever seen, mini binoculars. Now Gio remembered what had happened to his last top, and he liked the look of his new top, so in the spare of the moment he had an idea. He was going to smash these glasses to bits, but he hesitated, something inside of him took pity on this man and his megarims. He simply grabbed them off his head and stashed them in his jeans. "Aye, ye cheeky scouse cunt, give us, a can't see without 'em". Gio simply grabbed the man's tracky top and pulled it over his head. This looked so funny, Gio knew that he must finish off this move with a masterpiece. The man was staring into space, like he was concentrating on focusing. Gio swivelled round him and kicked him right up the arse. He simply overbalanced and was unable to use his arms to brace his crash to the concrete. "bastard" is all he heard as the leader crashed to the floor. A few of the lads were watching and the Leeds crew knew that their leader was incapacitated, and started to retreat from the superior numbers. There was something violently cool about this Liverpool mob, they just did things on the fly without thinking, it was the way they were brought up, it's how they got along and survived in an loaded society. The scousers chased off the rest of the boot boys, a few stones flew back at them. Gio then grabbed hold of the leader and gave him his glasses back, fully intact. "Sorry mate, I didn't want you busting my nose, your lot have scarpered up the runway."
"Nice one scouse, them cockneys would have left me for dead, up that way, yeh. See yeh."

The leader ran after his deserted mob and the boys all looked happy. This was turning out to be a top day. Just QPR to face off now. The next train was absolutely packed and the lads just squashed in, there was no room for messing about but a chorus of "Sardines, sardines, we're all sardines" was sang. As this mob turned up at Wood Lane station they noticed a few spotter rats for the Rangers. They were really young. "Fuck, its boo boo and yogi, robbin' peoples sarnies", Fergo shouted as they chased the young upstarts up the road. It was time to find a pub and there was a few about. But before the lads decided to make a visit to the BBC studio's as they had already saw this stunt done before and they wanted a bit of publicity. The 30 of them marched towards the edge of BBC TV centre and started looking over every wall until they found what they were looking for. Every one of the lads jumped over the wall and they were in the Blue Peter garden. They proceeded to tear up plants and splash each other with muddy water. Eventually John and Gio wrote LFC boys in the grass by using a trowel that was left around. Somebody had noticed them and the alert went out. "Fuck their gonna get shep the dog to lick us to death, let's go." The lads started laughing at Remo's jibe. "Those only one John Nokes, one John Nokes." Rod wasn't happy about the flowers being trampled as his mum loved her gardening, but he was sulking in quiet. "Valerie is a slag, Valerie is a slag, na nar nan na", the boys were now picking on poor old singleton. Some guard ran down with an Alsatian dog but the last of the lads was getting over the wall. The last comment was John who shouted "Fuck of Saville cuddling all the kids, ye fuckin paedo".

The lads walked down South Africa Road and started lobbing each other through some big privets. Then a big load of tenement blocks looked a big moody as there was all sorts of eyes on them. Now after four fights on the way the scouser's were a bit jaded and it didn't look like they fancied another ruck, unless they were inside the ground.

2

The 70's an education in violence and lifestyle

In order to be a Road Ender you needed to have gone through an initiation. This was basically the 1970's as a kid, and all the wonderful, colourful wild and violent things this decade had to offer.

The 1970s was full of airheads, Birmingham bag wearing wools (who also wore 3 star jumpers) and never cut their greasy heads. The music was shit, re hashed rock and roll and watered down folk music. The world was a wild place for teenagers, who seemed to live outside like feral rats. In the woods (and there were a lot of them then). The streets were not as busy, so basically the estates where a playground where kids kicked balls, and practiced fighting one another.

There was a city which was in a massive declining state, but so was most of the country. Technology was a word for the future, and the families were lucky to have a telephone, a coloured telly and a fridge. So, the only thing to do was hang around the streets. There were no social networks, to talk and brag about what you've got or what you are doing. No, you simply had to go out and do it, then think about it when you got older. One football team seemed to be dominating the world, when we won the European cup in 77 the streets erupted into song and kids ran through all the estate streets trailing big red and white scarfs and the blues stayed in, cursing their damn fathers for burdening them with having to watch the glory boys outside. It was a year after the scorcher, the hottest year ever. The big teams were Leeds and Ipswich, how the world has changed.

Violence was part of the 70's and 80's and if you didn't learn to use it you would be at a distinct disadvantage.

The 80's was a colourful decade, full of different types of music and teenage culture was absolutely massive and varied. During our teenage years we all got involved in lots of scrapes, even outside of the country.

One such event happened during a school holiday to Austria. At a young age your bigotry tendencies come out. As the crew of five lads walked through the scenic village of Seaham they let rip with a few choruses of "We won the war". The history teacher must not have been much good, as Austria switched sides eventually This mountain village was not used to English kids and didn't deserve these little rascals. Gio was 15 and didn't really like who he was on holiday with, he was put in a room with the school idiot. The idiot started the singing, and kids usually follow what one idiot does, and become a bunch of idiots. Each night the English were out the locals would close their shutters, and god knows what the teachers were doing. But teenagers will be teenagers and these lads were looking for fun without any access to alcohol. Instead the teenage rascals would get their first taste of something for nothing by self-pouring the coke machine in the lobby which was not supervised. Four local lads were still offended for being blamed for their German cousin's fascist tendencies, and decided to go and speak to the English to explain that "it wasn't them, or their parents fault."

However Mansley had seen the sound of music and just thought of these lads as Hitlers youth.

"What you saying about the war , man".

Mansley was undeterred "We won it, you never did, that's what I'm saying".

"My father was forced into fighting, we didn't want the war."

"Not my fault mate." Mansley stupidly replied.

"No war for 40 years, why are you bringing this up, stupid Englander. You come to our home and tell us how to live."

With that last statement the Austrian took offence and launched a karate kick straight into Mansley's midriff. Instead of helping, Gio and the other two lads started laughing at Mansley gulping on the floor. Another Austrian then decided to lamp Gio, who wasn't expecting anything, he thought this was just a one on one matter. He took a smack in the ear, and heard instant ringing and low volume. The other two lads sprung into action. One lad was called Roger and didn't seem the type to fight, but he knew he had to put up some sort of resistance. Gio was now offended as these lads were wearing Puma and Mitre trainers, and crappy sports tops. Gio had his Kio's on, Mansley a nice pair of Pod and Roger some groovy red kickers. Gio whacked this lad back straight in the kisser. His lip exploded. The karate kid was waving his arms around, pretending to be Bruce Lee.

"Come on! Bastards", Roger spurted out. It sounded nervous and strained, Roger was obviously struggling with violent tendencies. The fight petered out with a few nasty words here and there, and the Austrians saying "We can bring knives". It looked like these country boys were not quite as innocent as they looked.

Ste chipped in with "fuck off you woolies, with your crappy clothes. Fuck off back and milk your goats".

The rest of the holiday went by with the threat of the locals coming back with knives but nothing ever happened. A group of the lads had brought a union jack and used to go out for a few hours every night with it draped around their shoulders singing England songs. There was also an altercation on rowing boats but it's not even worth talking about.

The early decade was dominated by great synth bands like OMD, Depeche mode, Kraftwerk and tears for fears. The styles of the Huyton boys didn't really reflect the pop music. There was always one tosser with spikey shoes on or strange long duffel coats, or human league hair, but generally all the lads dressed the same. Usually black adidas trainers, Samba or mamba depending on how well off your parents were. Kickers, Kios or pods were usually worn. There was influences from the mods, the two-tone scene and the football lads. Generally, most lads liked the scally look, as it made you look and feel hard.

It was always a challenge getting around during an evening in the town. There wasn't much to do, it seems even now that our parent's generation didn't think about what teenagers needed. We were left to our own devices, some lads even tried glue as it was cheap and available for a quick kick. Eventually we all veered towards cider with Rosie. So, standing outside the "out door" was order of the day with a couple of quid hoping that the good nature of a passer-by would take pity on our terrible situation of being 15 and bored. The local chippy was another place to reduce our boredom, but that was usually quite dangerous. Remo and Rod were out on the street corner knocking a ball about. A few other lads were out there when this lad who seemed to get his style from his dad walked down the drive. Remo looked over "Your dad leave his Ted clothes out did he Noggin".

Noggin took offence and ran straight over to Remo and lashed out with a dog lead he carried for protection. It caught Remo right across the back and the end whipped with a crack. "you fuckin' Ted." Remo lashed out, with his fists and Noggin took the full force across his face. He was smashed against the floor and a couple of the lads pulled Remo off him. Noggin legged it back up the street and must have called his cousins mates who turned up ten minutes later in a jazzy car. It was an Asian lad, who were few and far between in this area. This lad had electric windows which was impressive in 82. "You lads want trouble" he asked. Everybody was stunned that anybody would come to their corner with such a cheeky request. They thought he must have something up his sleeve or a weapon of some sort. Nobody knew what to make of it. Then he had the audacity to look at Eddie and say "Are you soft of something?". Eddie simply replied with a nonchalant "Soft as putty mate". The Asian man simply drove off, not expecting no response from these Huyton street lads. Even the lads were stunned that they had for once frozen, and they never did this again. It was a lesson learned. Later that night Remo, Rod and John walked over to the Longview chippy. This involved traveling over a muddy field without any light. Everybody took a shortcut across that field even if it made you full of mud, teenagers were simply too lazy to walk in pre-determined squares. As soon as the boys could see sight of the shops they knew they had made a mistake. There were about 20 Longview lads throwing bottles at each other, some friends they were.

There was on skin head ironically called skinner who was left from the 70's the rest were just all scallies, in trackies and trainee's.

As soon as they laid eye's on the three lads, they got territorial. It was only ¾ a mile across the field but it still constituted as some sort of divide.

"You'se from Mozzy, what the fuck d'you want here?" The old skin head seemed to command some sort of respect from the scallies.

"Were only after chips and curry lad, what's the problem?"

"You're on our turf lad, fuck off back across that field, or we'll twat you".

The three lads knew they had no choice but to go to their own chippy which had scabby chips.

There and then they turned on their heels, but it was probably a mistake to submit so quickly.

"Yeh fuck off back to Mozzy you scruffs, and stop coming over here for our birds."

The lads kept their mouths shut. Rod didn't like being called a scruff as he was probably the best dressed lad in his street.

"Cheeky cunts" he mouthed but unfortunately it was loud enough for them to hear.

The roar went up and the three lads were on their toes.

Rod still had his Walkman on and an earphone in one ear and as he was running the music was knocked on. Now he didn't know whether this was fate but it started playing "What you give is what you get" by the Jam. The words sang "What you give is what you get". The music fired him up and he ran a little faster and gave a little grin to himself.

The lads behind them were giving it monkey noises and screaming sounding like something out of clockwork orange. This would be nasty if they were caught. John got to the old boxing hut and knew he couldn't outrun these lads as he scrambled onto the roof and hoped that they couldn't see what he was doing. He got on the roof and quickly lied down. The loonies were still after the two others and had totally ignored him, as the moon wasn't out and it was really dark. Some looney chasing didn't realise he was in a penalty box and it was really muddy, he went down straight onto his face. Some of the loonies started high pitched laughing. Remo and Rod scrambled through a gap in the railings, and looked back. They jumped over the old stream and up the hill of the CF Mott campus grounds. They looked back again and could see what looked like the antil mob trying to get through this little gap one by one. It was really slowing them down and half of them still had ciggies, which scrapped sparks through the nights as they hit the railings. As the next set of railing were reached Rod knew they had started to gain on him so didn't have time to take the railing carefully, one spike went straight through his hand. Behind the corner houses on Hurst Park Drive there was a back lane where they were able to climb over the fence at number 7 and hide in an outside toilet. The gang were flummoxed as they entered the back lane. There was still a fire burning there from some scally exploits earlier in the day. The Longview scallies decided to grab some burning logs and throw them over the fences of all the nearest houses to try to piss off the lads and their neighbours. A cat squealed as it was hit by burning sticks.

"Come out, and face your fate." One lad shouted, it was almost like being in clockwork orange or the Warriors.

Rod and Remo nervously laughed. Rod got through to the front road and knocked for a few of his mates, but he just couldn't get enough just yet. Remo did the same and after ten minutes there was ten of them. Worth a kick off they thoughts.

The Longview lads had now settled in and started setting fight to wooden garages to keep warm. The Mosscroft lads blocked off the entrance to the back lane and grabbed all the bricks, stones, asbestos and slate they could find. Just then a massive bang went off, it would be some asbestos roofing that everybody used to throw on the bommies to make a homemade explosion. Time for a stone fight, as half of Whiston Lane lads then joined in the fun. Bricks, logs everything was thrown at them and they were cornered and they knew it. But there was no shortage of ammunition by the Longview lads who launched a barrage of stones back. One slate skimmed through some bushes as smashed into some poor scally standing just behind it, gashing his cheek open. Then the Longview lads made a dash for it to the entry. "come on" they shouted. Rod's Walkman was now playing Eton Rifles, he was proper buzzing especially when the song said "Guilty schoolboy". The Longview lads escaped with a few kicks and punches on the way out. They knew they were not on their patch and would soon be outnumbered. The Mosscroft boys gave chase and they were soon all back by the Boxing hut. John jumped down after throwing a few bricks at them. And joined the little crew. Now that everybody was out Remo wanted to take on the Bakers Green lot, but everybody was knackered. They all went back to their street and started to kick a ball around again, to the annoyance of the local parents who always shouted "There's a big field over there and all you do is kick the ball against our walls, don't you ever go on that field, it will keep you out of mischief". The lads all knew they were in charge in this street, and if they were disturbed then they would just get into worse mischief.

Bombfire night was always lively around our area. Each street would have its own massive wooden igloo, which some kids would live in to stop other kids robbing their wood. It was a night of mayhem and kicks. Some of the fires were far too big, and would quickly burn out of control and set other fences alight. Some loonies would throw bangers into peoples' porches and ring the bell, some even embedded in dog shit, to make a foot-stamp possible. A few wooden garages went up every bommy night and sometimes the poor fire brigade to bricked for no apparent reason. This one bommy night Gio and John were on their way home from a shopping trip. It was going to be a day for watching your back and vandalism. As the bus got to Kensington two younger lads were behind them and this is what they said and did.

One lad was a bit of a scruff and was intent on mischief " Jeff get it done, have it lad, I just want to see it go up".

His mate Jeff was trying his hardest to set the seat alight, then they heard ripping and guff guff laughing from the thick vandals.

"It's on fire, ha ha, we did it" one of the lads was really enjoying his arson attempt.

Then he started coughing his guts up as he was still watching his little fire and directly ingesting the plastic fumes. It probably couldn't have made his brain any more ineffective as he was already fascinated by flames. Then he picked up a piece of plastic off the seat and held it in the air. The burning plastic started making fizzing noises as it dropped plastic bomblets onto the floor which carried on burning and giving off black smoke. What he didn't realise was that his coat had caught light. His two mates were laughing as they could see exactly what was happening. They did that silent, sneaky laughter that was contagious. Then he jumped up and cried out "No, my arm, my back, aaahhhhhh". His first mate threw a can of coke contents straight at his coat but he moved and it hit him in the face. By this stage he was waving his arm around trying to flap the flames out. The boys couldn't stop laughing, and another can then hit the target. As everybody was pre-occupied with poor Jeff's adventure nobody noticed the flames curling up the seat. Then it was apparent that the fire was out of control and everybody moved forwards about six seats, which really wasn't that wise. One lad opened the windows as black putrid smoke was bellowing from the seat.

Them days there was no CCTV on the busses so the driver was relying on the good will of the passengers if anything was wrong. There was a mirror by the front seat that the driver could see through, but they hardly ever used them. The newly created breeze fanned the flames. As the bus reached Old Swan some clever kids would add to the mayhem. Anyone who has ever been to Old Swan would know that it is Liverpool's biggest bottleneck. The buses are always stopped for ages. The gang around them parts were renowned and called the Swans. They were lining up by the shops and having fun by throwing fireworks and stones at passing cars. Two bricks went straight through the downstairs window followed by a banger. The passengers panicked and all tried to move upstairs, about ten pensioners and two young girls charged up the stairs, the bangers exploded, then they ran down again. It was like a Laurel and Hardy comedy scene. The top deck was like a fireman's prop, the whole front six seats were aflame. The bus jerked to a stop and everybody got off, even the driver ran away from it. A crowd of shoppers watched the whole bus burn out because the fire brigade were obviously too busy dealing with little brick throwing yobs around the city.

When there was nothing left, the fire brigade arrived. They were so surprised that the petrol tank hadn't exploded, but the driver explained that it was almost dry as they were told to use not much diesel that night just in case.

Gio and John jumped the next bus but wouldn't let the arsonists get on.

School barnies and watered-down sectarianism, Billy's not so smart circus and the school riot and school disco.

It was 1979 The latest music was a moody tune called 'ghost town' and everybody seemed to connect with the lyrics as nothing much happened in Huyton, unless you wanted a fight. This was the night of the school disco and it was an exciting time for 13 year olds feeling their way into life. Gio had union jack socks and he wanted all the girls to know how cool he was, but there was just too much competition, too many hard lads, so he couldn't catch the eyes of the pretty girls. He had to make do with listening to music and a little bit of flirting while the bad boys had their eyes the other way. Spandau Ballet was playing at the disco which went great but it was time to go home and back to school the next day. On the way to school there was an old gate, and you could take a short cut through the vale, and past the Catholic school. all kids love shortcuts, it's the laziness in them. As Gio and Alec walked down the shortcut, they got bricked by the Catholics. They threw a few back then got chased. As they reached their playground, they shouted The Guzzies are attacking. The protestant school rallied and the two mobs met in the middle of a tennis court. Bottles and bricks were thrown each way and there was a stand-off. Eventually two of the cocks from each school met up as they seen this battle as pointless because nobody was ever going to win. They wanted to go anti-establishment and rage against the system and adults. Two lads had but big A for anarchy signs stitched to the back of their blazers. For a few seconds it looked like the protestants who had bravely walked into the catholic school playground were going to get tonked. But they came back and brought with them the whole of the catholic school, girls and boys. It was a dangerous move but the whole two schools had not yet gone in for the nine o'clock form. They decided to start running and they ran down Huyton Hey Road towards the town centre, or what they called the Village. As they got onto the main road, it was just like a football crowd. There must have been close to a thousand kids, and this only meant one thing. As they started cheering a riot ensued. They started by raiding the little shop by the railway bridge then moved on towards the local estate. They found the poor milkman who was cowering in his little float. Loads of kids took bottles of milk off his float started to drink it then throw the bottles at the local house windows. When there was only a few bottles left they started to push each side of the float and surely but slowly it started to tip over. The police sirens sounded but this only made them more in the mood to riot. They cheered and screamed and headed towards the main shopping centre. Blue lights and police vans started arriving, but there was a few punks and skins among the school kids, then the older kids arrived. The eighteen and nineteen year olds got wind of what was going on. They all charged towards the village and some police had to run away there was so many youths. The girls were joining in the spirit of anarchy and punk rock. Loads of windows went through, just blind vandalism for the sake of it, for the sake of anarchy.

Old women with head scarves and shopping bags scrambled out to the way and then the kids raided the sweet shops, and grabbed everything they could, one lad even thought to rob the till. Then sports shop pride and joy got raided. About sixty lads ran in and stole all the shoes, which was stupid as they only had left shoes displayed. Some kids tried and failed to put two left shoes on. Some lads had nabbed a west ham top but got smacked a few times so decided to dump it. Even the dogs ran away, then finally there was a stand-off with the police. The whole of the pedestrianized area was swollen full of school kids. There was no way they could all be arrested so the police tactic was to surround them then march them back to the schools. Eventually they calmed down after throwing a few missiles at the police and singing "Oh no, we won't go". Finally, the main teachers arrived, and for some psychological reason the kids did what the teachers said simply because that was the order of things in the world, in the end that is what they were used to.

But the mood of youth was far from over that day. On the local field between the estates the gipsy's had decided in their wisdom to host a massive circus with real animals, actual lions and elephants. Now gipsies are renowned for being hard cases and can look after themselves. But they defiantly chose the wrong town the host a circus at just the wrong time. They spent the whole day trying to stop kids robbing off them, bit of an irony there. Loads of people bunked in, and to make things worse somebody let the elephants lose. Granada reports turned up and the kids were seen chasing the elephant around the field. The north side of the tent was set on fire for five minutes and the gypsi's were really fed up with if all especially when the lions started to get irritated by the kids poking sticks at them and telling them to "fucking come on, lets av ye lion". The national press arrived and it's the only time we have ever saw a lot of gypsi's being grateful for the police moving them on. They never came back to that town ever again.

3

YTS hooligans

In 1983 the strange feeling after leaving school was like a void. You were expected to go on the dole, or go on the dole. There was simply NO work, and some tory toff told us to get on a bike and abandon our home, so we didn't. We went on YTS schemes instead. For £25 a week, and a good bit of work experience that stood us in good stead. It gave you a work ethic, or it should of if the work wasn't so scarce. One scheme was just like a teenage hangout. This is what happened in one of these dusty, smelly old welding factories called Huyton Training Workshop. There was a big crew of local lads all 16 and trying to get a foot up in life, but they all knew that this was just another Tory plot to keep us off the streets for a few extra quid, which we used for Friday and Saturday boozing. As one of the lads used to say "We live for the weekend, because we don't have anything else to look forward to".

"Hey Evo, What you up to? Where we going today" Davo was a good feller but from a tough family.

"We're going down Anfield to fit up some shop doors, reckon they'll be a kick off with the Breck Road lot".

"Yeh I reckon, you got any draw for the trip lad?"

"Nah, we picked some magic mushies though, we can do them in."

Gio was on his own, but some other lad called Lango was on the scheme and he had started hanging around at the match with the other nutters.

There was no such thing as being safe and healthy in them days, the main scheme runners just threw all the lads in the back of a red van, and off they went, sitting on the doors they were to fit, down to Breck Road in Anfield. As they unloaded a few gangs were watching them.

Some lad with a black track suit walked over and started watching them.

"Ey lad, were are you'se lot from, are you wools from Prescot or Maghull?"

"No lad, ye cheeky cunt, we're from Huyton, now you better fuck off if ye gonna abuse us by calling us wools, if ye want a go, go and bring ye boys, we'll fuckin' do ye." Lango was having no trouble off these bunch of blue nose County Roaders, or whoever they were.

The lads started to fit and weld the doors into the shop-ways when a bunch of scramble bikes careered towards them, one lad had an iron bar and as he went past he caught Booty right on the legs. He flew off the ladder in agony and you could see his leg was snapped in two. The supervisor quickly made a splint and threw him in the van leaving the whole crew of Huyton teenagers to take on the Breck Road lot. There was seven of them on scramblers, not one of them had a helmet on. Gio and Lango took the lead as they were now not scared to get stuck in with anyone. As they came past again with their fists clenched and v signs, Gio charged at one and booted the bike, he didn't know how he did it but it didn't half hurt his leg, he didn't count for the speed of the bike which jarred him right back. Anyhow the rider went flying and smashed into a bin. The scramble boys didn't expect a kick attack and all the trainees cheered. The lad was not getting up for a while, they all thought it served him right for not wearing a helmet. The next pass came without a problem but the bikers were spitting as far as they could. The next pass the trainees were ready and launched all sorts of bricks and old branches at the motorbikes. Another one skidded and the two lads fell off. They tried their hardest to get it started again as they were un injured but the Huyton lads were on them like a pack of wolves, kicking fuck out of them. Lango put his hand up and said they've had enough and let them crawl away but all the lads jumped on their damaged bike to make sure they couldn't attack anyone else. They all then jumped the 75 bus back home and spent the rest of the afternoon in the Rose and Crown pub, waiting for the night to arrive as there was a proposed CB night. This was one of them nights when all the CB'ers would meet up for what they called an eyeball. But it was just another excuse to meet girls and fight with other lads. As the different crews arrived from different parts of the town, it was all ok at first, but the mood started changing when the St Johns and the Page Moss lads started to snarl at each other. Before you know it this lovely old pub so full of mirrors had become a very localised riot. Glasses flew everywhere, the girls screamed and every window was put in. The two gangs charged at each other and blood spurted against the broken mirrors and lovely maroon seats.

4

The MIG's

One of the main pubs LFC fans used to frequent was on the corner of Breck Road, not too far from where I live now. During the noughties I used to DJ there and found out it was full of Everton's boys, who cheekily asked me "Are you a bizzy?", as I saw them sniffing some kind of pitch chalk in the bogs. "Nah, I wish I was on their money lad". The cheek of them lads taking over our pub. Anyway in the 80's the whole of Breck Road was a decent night out on a Saturday and Friday night. One Saturday afternoon (It always was a Saturday back then) The boys all met up before the match. Now a lot of them were still a bit skint in 83 and had to use their powers of robbery to get a drink.

Rod used to ask the barman for peanuts. He never stocked the cashews in the front of the bar. For some reason it was always down the cellar. Every time he went for some about ten lads would re-fill their pints. One time, Remo even managed to wedge his door wedge in there so they had a bit more time to refill. Debbie was a gorgeous barmaid who all the lads lusted after. She was about 22, with almost perfect figure. This one day they really went to town on the cashew nut trick. Debbie was laughing her tits off behind the bar and knew the bar manager was a bit dopey, hence the reason she worked here. She used to pilfer a little from the till for her new clothes shopping session every Friday.

"Al right Debbs, you seeing anyone yet", Remo thought himself a bit of a Romeo, when he saw a decent bird.

"What's it to you kid", Debbie was emphasising the slight age difference as Remo was still only 18.

"It's just there is a family party next week at me ma's place, an all nighter you know, thought you might like to come down and test a few cocktails I have made up."

"Check your cock what, sounds like a small task."

Remo looked embarrassed as her voice increased while answering.

The boys all started laughing and giving Remo winks.

"Remo's on the bag."

to the tune of one nil to the Liverpool they sang in unison "SMALL THINGS AMUSE SMALL MINDS."

Debbs couldn't help laughing and Remo came back to the lads. "Yeh Yeh, you've had your laughs, at least I got her number".

"Yes and she got yours, 5.5 inches" Rod laughed his answer.

The Ale was flowing and the wacky backy came out. It was Rods turn to be daft. Barney was a local lad from Breck Road. He was well into the violence scene and was a bit of an organiser where the reds had none. "Luton Town are in town today, there is a little crew called the MIGS, I don't know if they think they are Russian jet planes or mad men, but there may well be a kick off by the Arkles, Jez knows one of them and he has rang up last week asking for a kick off with us."

"Ye little spy Jaz, are these lads geared up or are they bovver knobs."

"Oh yeh, they're well geared up, they've been hanging round with Chelsea and got a few ideas off them."

Fuckin' plastic cockney's, I hate them all. Fancy pall'ing up with Chelsea, that's bad, it's like us and Man City getting together".

"I know, but I've got a plan to rag some gear off them, and to tax their wallets, they're full of reddies these southerners". The plan involved getting baiting them into Stanley Park and ambushing them. As the day drew on the boys realised they had started to drink a bit too early.

Remo was swinging from a light fitting, the bar manager was not happy but knew not to make too much of a fuss, or his windows might become un-waterproof.

Remo was making tarzan noises and kicking glasses off their tables. Some scarfer got ale all over him and didn't look happy, but knew who were the nutters so left it alone.

"Fuck this I'm a bit too pissed, time to go for a walk lads, lets see what's going down by the ground".

The boys were walking towards the Park pub, There was about five casuals who looked like they could be Luton MIG's. Barney walked over asking if they knew "Banksy from the MIGS". They got all on the defensive thinking that the road end boys were going to attack them. Two lads grabbed some bin lids and put them up in front of Barney. "I just wanna know lads, he promised a meet up by the Arkles. How many you lot got"?

One lad leaned over and tried to twat him with the bin lid. "No need for that lad, I was only asking a question".

Some cockney shouted "Fuck off scause, you want it".

The boys postured to jump across the road, but one lad shouted. "It's ok I know him, it's still on be we've only got 20, should be another 60 by half one".

"Alright lad, tell him, he's on then, we're ready for you gonks".

A couple of 'V' signs where waved and they Luton started to jog up the road.

The boys entered The Park pub, and a few of the lads were wary of drinking anymore, but they did, just like you do, when you are young and carefree.

The pub was a traditional type pub with a low ceiling, and rust coloured décor throughout. Dark wood panelling was everywhere, and so was Remo and Rod, both nearly off their shopping trollies. They began to slur their words as the next bevvy was served. "Show me the way to go home, cuz I'm tired and I wanna go to bed, FOR A WANK!, they're only half a football club, no match for the boys in red" Rod and Remo started singing with scarfers, because deep down we were all football fans and fans of Liverpool.

Now the drinking was getting out of hand and the next pub they jumped in was The Albert, it was a bit further up the main road. It was jam packed but it never deterred the boys and by now there was about 50 of them. A few scarfers scarpered with their pints when they saw who was entering, making just enough room for the gang of loonies to stand around. They had one of the junior wannabee's keeping an eye out down by the Arkles just in case the MIGS turned up early. Gio, John and Fergo had already had enough of drinking and decided with about 30 others to go down to the Arkles for a gander at what was going on. They decided to go in fives to deceive the police as these lads stood out like a sore thumb with their nice gear on. What they found when they turned the corner was an eye opener. They had taken a few steps around the corner and noticed about 60 Luton who had seemed to have taken control on the pub. The simple answer was all the boys were in the other pubs and they saw it as their right to take over.

Now Remo had earlier hatched a plan to lose the police, basically the lads up in the Albert were start a pretend fight, and smash a few windows. Now Remo was well up for this when he got the report from the Arkles spies, but him and Rod were really in a wild drunken mood.

"It's time Rod, it's time to blag the bizzies, let's get naughty". About 20 lads started to throw pints at every wall. Remo looked at the barman and grabbed a whole bottle of whisky "I've always wanted to do this since I watch the good the bad and the ugly", he lobbed the 1 litre bottle straight through a window. Rod looked up "Yeeeees, I'll have a go at that", Rod threw another at a 5 foot mirror it smashed to smithereens. "Another seven years on my bad luck book". The scarfers all ran for cover, and the sirens started to wine. The 20 lads all ran out at once, and over to the coppers. "It's the Luton MIGS, they've attacked us and ran into the back of the pub, they're in the yard copper". Doyley was on the case. As the pigs stormed the pub the 20 boys calmly walked away. Remo still had a bottle of vodka right behind his back and he was stumbling around the pavement. Rod was just laughing at him; he was somehow balancing what was left of his pint better than his legs, although he was spilling a bit. "Who the fuck are Luton, who the fuck are Luton, their plastic cock's, they're plastic cocks". Rod and Remo were singing anything that came into their heads again, they were in a world of their own, it was funny to them, and I think they meant plastic cockneys, but it sounded better.

The road end boys now numbered about the same as Luton who started fronting up outside the shop. There was only a small window of opportunity as the police raced around the corner to the Albert.

20 of them were now outside the pub with their arms up in the air, asking for it. They were jumping up and down egging themselves on for the fight to follow. The road end boys stormed into them and they got flattened against the wall. It was a ferocious attack, five Luton got butted in a row by the wall. More Luton piled out trying to re-enforce their numbers but it was like a real time strategy game where you couldn't build enough soldiers to cope with the onslaught. There was simply not enough room for them all to get out of the pub at once.

About five Luton lifted up a wooden bench with tables attached trying to break the attack but they were soon all smacked around the heads and hit the deck. The scousers got into them without any holding back, load of lads were getting kicked all over the floor, it was like a kicking contest to see who could get the most digs in. Those who got up quickly got smashed down again by eager fists. Then the Luton numbers coming out started to make some headway. They started to fight back, and they knew that they couldn't hold back. About five scousers went down and the focus of the battle moved towards them. Remo and Rod were still walking around the corner when they saw the action. They quickly sprung into life, adrenaline taking over from absolute drunkenness. Gio and John were getting stuck in, and John was swinging a Luton lad around by his jumper, the lad didn't know what to do but try to kick out so nobody would reach his face with a dig. He swung around about twice and they smashed into about 3 of his own crew. It seemed to be a brown Pringle but it now had a new opening at the bottom, somebody had slashed out with a craft knife while he was swinging, he was lucky it only slashed his jumper. "Raaazors, they've go razors", some Luton was shouting. About ten more lads stormed out and started throwing pint glasses, most of them half full at the scousers. One glass smashed on the back of Gio's head, he felt his head but there was no blood, not even a bump yet. It just motivated Gio to carry on fighting, and narked him a bit. Gio ran over to a black lad and ragged his hat off as a souvenir; the lad looked at him as to say 'take it then'. Gio then started to lash out with both arms and stormed into about three migs, who seemed to have a bat between them. They smashed it against Gio's ribs and probably broke about two. Gio went for the baseball bat as he didn't fancy any more smashes on his bones. He grappled and some lad punched him in the back of the head. Now this got his goat and he managed to find the strength to yank it off the lad and swing it around to his attacker. Gio smashed him right in the nose, his nose went everywhere. This was starting to become and epic battle. Rod and Remo stormed in together like a double force they co-ordinated their attack straight into Luton's ranks. The new momentum and insane strength gained from alcohol intake and the feeling of invincibility was the straw that broke the camel's back. Luton started to run, and straight down Anfield Road and towards the Flat Iron pub. About ten lads made a mistake of running down Edit Road, and some road enders had relied on Luton trying this route to the main road and the safety of the police. All the lads were in on it, and the 20 who had left the pub waited at the top for them to charge down. Luton looked around like caged animals and realised that they were trapped in a small terraced street. Three lads started banging on somebodies door to let them in, but the curtains were shut in disgust.

Some MIG tried to get in a car for his own safety, but a big heavy catalogue was thrown at him from a house window and hit him on the shoulder, so he retreated to underneath the car.

The ten lads saw him do this and thought it was their only form of protection. Remo and Rod shouted "Tax time!, lets rob the rich cockney bastards".

Rod and Remo grabbed the first lads by the legs "What size feet are you lad"? Remo asked. The cockney was surprised at the request and just told them he was a seven. "Shite, leave him", They went to the next lad "Shoe size cockney"? "What the fuck you want that for"? "Just tell us or we'll kick fuck out of you"? There was no negotiating with conquerors. "Size 9, size 9, don't twat me". "Sound lad", Rod yanked his trainers them off him, and looked in his plastic bag he had with him. He mouthed the words 'size 9' then pulled out some Dunlop green flash that were left over from the seventies, which his mum had bought him for after school. "Ey are lad, enjoy them, I never did". Remo actually put one on the lad's feet and shouted at him to wear them both. The lads ran to the next lad who had some nice red adidas Munich on. "Have you got any size tens mate"? Remo was likening the situation for being in Timpsons for some reason, he went all polite. The man nodded and Remo yanked them off his feet, but as he did this he noticed a nice pair of Tacchinni blue track suit bottoms. "Did you have a wash this morning lad"? The lad looked terrified and nodded. "Get them track suit bottoms off then and we won't attack ye again". The lad threw them at Remo who pulled some old Liverpool shorts out of Rods bag and threw them at him. "Support a proper team lad, one with history". The lad put the shorts on and Rod sorted through his shoes and pulled out some red sandals. "Here you go Cindy, lovely red shoes for the ball".

Gio, John and a few other lads had ragged some tracksuit tops, Adidas, Ellesse and fila off these lads and left them with their t-shirts and shirts on. Everybody got their trainers taxed, and Rod just threw his old shoes into the road, the MIGS walked over and started trying shoes on like old tramps with nothing to lose. The lads left them be, and nobody got any money robbed as that was deemed 'robbery' of the worst type, almost like mugging which they didn't do. John had a lovely ski bubble coat on now, it only just fitted him "These Luton have got some money, I was looking at one of these down the St John Market, it was over two ton la!". Gio looked up "You got a bargain lad".

The fight was re-invigorated down by the flat iron. The MIG's had all got back as one big group and were now ready to fight. From their rear were appearing the clothes orphans, who wanted revenge in their green flash.

Five mig's had those big thick heavy road cones ready to launch. Three lads had big pots lined up ready to sling at the scousers, and there were some pre thought gone into weaponry. They seemed to have supplied axe handles, which were extra hard so they never broke, like wooden bones. One lad had pulled a ladder from somebodys garden, the man was still on it at the time, but he soon scarpered to his back yard. They had broken up the ladder into pieces and about ten lads had a step each ready for clobbering the scouse hordes with.

The knife boys had gotten word about the fight and were now approaching their enemies with evil contempt and eager flick wrists. Some other MIG's had got into the flat Iron and robbed all of the glass cigarette trays. There was a standoff and the police were getting wind of what was going on. Only one van had arrived but they stood off waiting for re-enforcements. The 100 yards went down to 80 yards, then 70. Each side was ready to clash, Luton were bruised and angry but Liverpool had some nasty Stanley boys ready to tip the balance.

Like and England vs Scotland clash in Brave heart the North and South clashed. Remo got a ladder step smashed against his face and his nose busted open. He just carried on fighting with his la coste orange t-shirt ruined; it was always a sacrifice worth taking. Ten scousers took the lead but all got clobbered by weapons. Most of the lads just wanted to get their fists in cockney faces and swung wildly. Nobody was trained to fight; they only had their training growing up in tough estates and learned a few evil tricks. Fergo saw that weapons were out on the Luton side so used his little trick. He looked for one of the biggest casuals and launched a flying kick right at the middle of his calf between his knee and his food. His legs snapped instantly, and a few MIGS pulled back in shock. Everybody ignored him in agony and he was stood on by lads from both sides. The coppers saw that this was the height of fighting so they needed to get out, but the MIG's had used remains from the ladder to wedge the doors shut, and they were going ballistic trying to get out.

Gio and John stormed in again, but it was too little too late. The MIG's had the scousers running back on home turf, it felt like a travesty. Then the four Stanley boys stopped them in their tracks. Four lads in a row shiny blades for all to see. They had scarfs wrapped over their faces in case of any police id or cctv systems which were already installed on police vans. The cones all got thrown and a few pots which still had mud in. The mud seemed to stay where it was thrown from but the pots all landed just past the shoulders of the knife boys. Another surge towards the Stanley boys but the scousers had gotten their bravery back due to the nasty thread by them ahead. They got too close, but the force of lads behind pushed MIG's in to the Stanley boys who started to lash out. Some lad's bubble coat suddenly burst and he jumped to the side his aerated coat had saved him from some nasty scars. Five lads were not so lucky though and got the full force of the cutting crew. This gave the scouser hoards their advantage back and they started to lay into what was left of the MIG's. The Stanley boys melted back into the crowd, and the scousers were on the hunt. Three lads were stragglers who were being a bit too brave, got kicked all over the floor, but the bizzies were now on the ball. The van was broken open as they had to smash their own windows, and five more vans arrived, some coppers with dogs and coppers on horses.

They had missed all of the action, except the spectator coppers who had a full view of everything. There was a few injured MIG's on the floor, with a fair bit of blood about. Some of them coppers secretly liked to witness the violence but they usually don't like to admit it to anybody else. A good few punches by themselves usually satisfied their own violent tendencies and made them feel part of the battle.

When the battle was over, Remo and Rod were finished and simply toddled off back down the road and into the Sandon. Remo fell asleep while Rod lit up another spliff to wake himself up. Everybody went into the ground and nobody got arrested due to the police delay, and lack of evidence. A few poor cockneys were sent to hospital with superficial cuts and the police were on top for the rest of the match, so no more skirmishes occurred.

6

The wools

Football hooligan fights were often most vicious at derby matches, not so much in Liverpool, where everybody knew that the rest of the country were on their cases, so the best thing they could do would be to stick together. Huyton was full of fields and one field was a bit of a border between two local towns. The accent actually changed up in Prescot and the wools would come down for a barney every Saturday night. The grounds of the field were private and belonged to Liverpool University. On this balmy summers night the gangs of Huyton didn't want to go home. Some lads had broken into the campus and rolled 5 barrels of beer onto the field. They had also got hold of a bag full of magic mushrooms for afters. Remo, John, Rod and Gio were all out for the night in 1980 waiting for any sort of challenge from them 3 star jumper bermo boys from up the road.

Some nut had lit a fire by one of the ancient trees which was burning quite violently so the boys moved a few hundred yards and carried on supping the stolen Ale.

"Can't we sell these barrels, I need some cash la!" John was a little short this week and was always looking for ways for a fast earner.

"Nah, these will be gone by tomorrow, the lads on the estate know about them, there will be a forest party soon. I heard they were bringing some birds down with them." Gio was convinced he would get a good keg down himself the next few days.

"The fucking wools will try again you know, they like a bevvy as much as us. Half of the adults up there are on the dole as well."

They were all aged between 13 and 15 and still well up for some lager and cider if they could get it.

The area was private land but everybody bunked it, simply because they shouldn't be there, and there was a stream and some tree's, so everybody made tree ropes. Ten lads from Prescot descended on the camp, they had two tone baggies trousers on and 'v' neck wooly jumpers, and that's probably why they were called woollies Gio thought. "You got any money lads, or cigs". "Nah, Why would we give you money lad". Remo wasn't impressed. "Because I'm seventeen and I asked you twat". "Fuck off ye wool". The older lad instantly threw a brick that hit Remo on the face. His head started to leak blood, and John stood up. John was 18 and had a go at the bigger lad. That's when the mass brawl started. The lads from Huyton were half pissed and full of Dutch courage, but there was too many of the Prescot lads and they were too big. The chased lasted for five minutes and the Huyton boys ended up, up trees. The wools started lashing mud bombs at them. These consisted of reeds from the stream. By half an hour, they were covered in mud. They eventually got bored and went back up the Lane to their home town. As the lads got older they never forgot that one adventure, and you never forget a face who has attacked you, no matter how long ago. There was fourteen of the lads from the local estate in the Deans House in Prescot and in walked five of the same lads, but this time everyone was the same height and size. Remo latched eyes onto him and told Fergo to mind the door, in case they made a run for it. Remo was on the pool table with Rod and John and this lad just walked over and put his ten pence's on the table for a game. Remo made sure he won the next three games, even telling the lads he was playing to lose and he would sort them out with a flynn. When Wallace got to the table he looked at Remo with a slight bit of recognition. "Don't I know you lad?" Remo didn't even look at him "Ye might, or you will do soon." "What do ye mean by that?" Wallace looked concerned as he racked up the balls." Have you heard of the LFC boys". "No not really, I support saints, not into footy just Rugga". "Well, we're the boys who go the match, and I think I owe you one wool".

"What do you mean owe me one." Wallace had cottoned on to something was about to kick off and he called over his mates with his hand. It looked like Remo only had three mates and Wallace fancied his chances.

"Didn't you used to come down the CF Mott campus, to pick on Huyton boys in the seventies lad".

Now Wallace knew something was about to happen and he was unsure why Remo was so sure about himself.

"Rugby is shit mate, its men feeling each other for points".

Wallace didn't say nothing, but carried on wafting his mates over. Then there was five of them. One was a skinhead, the others were semi-scallies with gear you could get in the cheap sports shops. Remo looked up, "I like your Hi-Tech shoes mate, did your grandma get you them for Christmas." Hi-tech boy picked up a pool cue. Remo looked at another lad "Le coq sportif, were you abandoned as a kid and went looking for clothes in skips". With that the lad took offence and launched a fist straight at Remo. Remo ducked then whistled. The boys all came storming in from the other room where they were told to hide out. Wallace swung for his life, his punches were thrown like he was still a seventeen year old, and had practiced on a punch ball, these lads were not battle hardened. Remo smashed a stool right over his head and he went down like a hore. A big tall skinny lad looked around and panicked, he launched a bottle which landed straight at Rods chest, but didn't break as it was one of them half pint bottles. It fuckin' hurt Rod though, which just made him that little bid madder. He fully arched his arm and smashed another bottle on this lad's head. The lad grabbed his head and ran out the door, his exit blocked, he tripped up but barged his way through, nobody wanted to get blood on them. The bar manager was shouting "NO! NO!" having previously had his bar smashed up only weeks before. The dart board was pulled off and lashed like a Frisbee at the wools. The last of them ran out shouting "Saint's will come and have you". Remo had not forgot and grabbed a plant pot from outside. As Wallace looked up he poured the whole plant all over him and said "Scores are even wool, now go and get a fucking shower."

Isle of man

A lot of lads in 80's Liverpool had to move away to find work. One surprising location was the Isle of Man. In the 70's this was a holiday destination but it quickly became a tax haven, and scouse girls were encouraged to emigrate for the hotel trade. The Liverpool lads were encouraged to stay away, as the islanders knew what they were like, however this didn't stop Gio, Jon and Abbo. The easy passage on the boat was a deciding factor, together with sisters who worked on the island.

In Lancaster Station, the ghetto blaster was blasting away 80's hits and Beatles classics. Passengers looked on with discord at the young hoodlums. There was also a few Preston fans boarded who were travelling up to Carlisle for some game or other. Twelve Preston casuals walked straight down the carriage, they had a quick look around and noticed how the scousers were dressed. As they all walked past looking for a bigger mob to fight, one mouthed "We'll be back". Abbo mouthed back "if ye like".

"Fuck Abbo, what ye doing, there's loads of them", John looked a bit concerned as he knew what they would need to resort to, to sort out 12 lads. They all grabbed any weaponry they could find. Abbo broke a bottle under the table, John pulled a leg off an adjoining table despite protests from a pensioner. "Stick the beastie boys on Abbo, and maybe some punk. That will get us in the right frame of mind".
Abbo did as he was told, but some traffic announcement thing kept coming on and ironically saying there may be stormy seas today. It looks like the Preston may have found someone else to pick on further up the train, so the boys relaxed a little, there wasn't far to go until Heysham and their Lancaster stop

off.

"What even division are they in, I can't believe they've got boys", Abbo started.

"Everyone's got boys now Abbo, even Tranmere". The same old woman who was bad-eyeing the youths pulled her bag from the top storage compartment, but it tumbled to the table with a loud thud. John jumped with nervous excitement.

Then six of the Preston returned and stopped in front of the scousers.

"What do you lot want? And why didn't you bring yer full crew, you'll need them". Gio gestured towards the other door.

"You'se scousers think you own it, where ever you go, we outnumber you two to one, we don't need the rest", with that statement the lad in shorts with tattooed legs swung for Gio and smashed his nose. John seen it coming and already had hold of the old woman's bag. He swung it in an arc, it landed like a beauty straight into tattoo boys face, who went down in an instant. Another swing at Gio and John, they were badly outnumbered. John pulled out his smashed bottle and everyone else jumped out of their seats and started running to another carriage. John swung a warning with his bottle in an arc. The Preston were stunned by this show of force and didn't realise they were picking on another football mobs core soldiers. Abbo swung again, this bag must have had bottles in or something, and it knocked another lad clean out. The old woman stayed in her seat as she obviously wanted her bag back, maybe to sup whatever alcoholic drink she had in it. But the battle was far from over as Gio pulled his chair leg out and started to swing with that. The boys were putting up a good fight but if the others came they would be badly outnumbered and needed an escape plan. Lucky for them, a bridge came into view outside, as they approached Lancaster station. They all charged for the door and Abbo threw the old woman's bag at the hoolies who gave it straight back to the old woman. John jammed the carriage door as Gio struggled to open the outside door. The train must have been doing 30mph as the rest of the Preston crew arrived. Time for a sharp exit, as all three jumped into some thick looking grass. Abbo's getto blaster was still attached to his arm, and jarred his arm as it landed. They all did about three or four rolls as they hit the grass. They looked up and Preston were out of every window shouting profanities at them.

"fuckin ell lad, this is like being in an old American western film, mad or what?"

John was stunned by what they just did. They quickly found a country road and were glad that they had already transverse the river. They saw two pretty girls and asked directions to the station. "Over the hill, over the next hill, then turn right, straight up the lane." John was tempted to ask the country girls to walk them, but Abbo had already started off on the trek to Lancaster. The three lads encountered a pub and asked the locals for direction. One man actually had a pony in the pub with him, which the lads found amusing, it had some sort of eating bucket attached around its mouth a shit collector thing on its arse. These wools will do anything for a quick pint. As the lads hit the boat to Douglas the music started to blur and the weather was taking a turn for the worse. Nevertheless pints were the order of the day, and as the boat moved so did everybody else, more so after more pints.

There was a rugby team coming over from Leicestershire.

They were big lads but it didn't deter John and Gio from taking the mikey. They were also all drinking heavily and singing filthy songs.

The lads approached them. "How can you sing filthy lyrics like that in front of all of these kids" John was asking why they had no morals even though the casuals always sang whatever next entered their mind without a thought for families in the football stadium.

"Who are you mate, we're the good players of Leicestershire district league, and we can sing what we want".

John was really worst for wear now and decided he had the high moral ground and didn't like posh cunts.

"Why do you play with your funny shaped balls? What's wrong with normal balls"?

Some of the big rugby lads were getting irritated, but were unsure about these casuals and if they were carrying or had extra lads dotted about the boat.

John carried on as Gio was laughing his balls off "Why do you lads always jump on each other and hug each other? Bunch of fucking big pansies."

John laughed in one big lads face and he took exception. He jumped up and went to go at John but one lad who must have been the captain shouted him down, then gave him those I'm your dad eyes. He quickly backed down. Them lads must have been on strict orders to behave, maybe because of a previous altercation. Anyway, John and Gio were lucky that day, as 12 against two just doesn't go even when you feel invincible.

In Douglas the lads found work hard to come by but made the most of it anyway. When they ran out of cash they started to steal from the local stores. It was £15 for a week in lodgings with mouldy ceilings. They did have a few run ins with some bikers, one was in the Central bar. Abbo was drunk this day and there was a man who was conning people by asking them to ride his bike just ten yards. Loads of drunks were trying and failing. Abbo was sure he could do it, and tried three times. The problem was he was drunk, the wheel would turn left as you turned the handle bars right. It was natural instinct to turn the right way to balance, it was an ingenious idea to fleece the drunks of their hard earned cash. Abbo failed to the amusement of his friends, and spent five quid trying to prove them wrong. As they entered the Central bar later that night, they sat in the corner where they thought they wouldn't be disturbed.

These bikers were another breed and the girls they had for company were well kinky wearing all sorts of black fish net stockings and dark kinky make up. Short leather skirts with suspenders, the lads were like hot dogs, with their tongues hanging out, waiting for a chat up line to enter their minds.

Some musclebound man with a dodgy black vest with AC/DC printed on it approached the lads. "You fancy a bit of that". He was obviously a Northerner but was trying to put a yank tone into his accent. "Ye not wrong mate, there is things I could do to these women, that wouldn't get in a porno." John was getting more desperate with the more ale he drank.

"Well you won't go near them lads, cuz these are our girls. You go and get some girls in pink or girls in track suits, get me."

"Fuck off, ye smelly bastard, we'll have whoever we want, were not desperate we are scouse."

"I know a lot of heavies in here, and what we say goes, we are dangermen, we rule this island".

"Fuck off danger mouse, and go and get your heavies, we'll see what you can do."

The man fucked off and John looked at Gio and Abbo with a bit of fear in his eyes. "I think we might have bitten off more than we can chew again lads, shall we fuck of back to Castlemona Avenue to watch the moss grow on the ceilings." The lads swilled up and walked around the corner. They were still on the corner of the prom when ten bikers motored down the prom and one pointed at them. They all instantly done donuts, changed direction and headed for the scousers. The lads jumped over a wall and knelt down looking through the bars of the concrete wall that was also a concrete fence. The bikers motored up Castlemona then down again looking for the lads. The next pass there was less of them. Then there was just three. "We can take these now there is equal numbers, fucking smelly bastards, let's do them." The scousers jumped out as they made their next pass. Abbo did something fantastic, something nobody has seen done before. As the biker came past he noticed Abbo but was too late to stop the attack. Abbo simply held his fist out as the bike passed. The bikers only had half helmets on, one of them a German war helmet. Abbo caught the earlier protagonist square in the face, he must have been doing 30 miles per hour. It looked like slow motion as he hit his face, the bike seemed to carry on and the biker slowed down instantly. It was amazing how his body was faster than his head. He did a backwards summersault and skidded along the road. His nose exploded. Abbo was laughing his bollocks off and Gio and John were just amazed at what they saw. The other two bikers simply went to help their mate, and the lads never had any more trouble with the bikers again, during their whole stay on the island. Their stay on the Island was cut short by some sort of rule that said you couldn't stay there if you were male and not from the island.

8

Celtic Away

Some people say that "Violence undermines and yet holds up society".

There's a Rage that burns
In my veins
A rage that burns
And it stains.
There's a rage that fires
Up my soul
And sometimes makes
Me feel whole

There's a fire that does
Not go out
There's a fire that
Keeps me afloat
There's a fire that
Lights my way
It's a fire that
Makes me pay

There's an anger that
Forever grows

An anger that
Always knows
Where I was
When I was young
The fire that started
Fills like sponge

So where did the anger of the youth come from.
Was it a lack of impurities in food that gave us more testosterone? No, it
couldn't have been because half the girls were fighting each other.
Was it inequality with the middle classes? No because hardly any of us knew any
middle classes they all lived in a different world in garden cities down South.
Was it born out of boredom? Not really, we had plenty to do, but possibly was a
factor.
Was it because there were no politically correct rules, that made you feel guilty
if you done something different from the robot masses of the internet age.
Because you did things on a whim out of independent thinking and curiosity.
Was it because we wanted to find out what it was like to be alive, and what it
felt like to get chased with the prospect of real danger. You make your mind up,
mine was already decided in that great decade.
It was the decade of New. New things like fads that were made by the teenagers
themselves and not some corporate image designers. An angry type of music
made by angry teenagers. We were angry because the adults let us be angry.
There was a new type of kid. A kid who didn't have to worry about going down a
mine or going to university to learn pointless shite that meant nothing to them.
Some of us were to be the forgotten generation, and we knew what was
coming. When the tories got into power, does anybody think that it was just
racism by the police that provoked the riots of the early eighties. No, it was
started by the blacks as a protest against bigoted police, but it was carried on
and expanded by angry teenagers who seen the writing on the wall. The writing
that said 'You are the ones who will have to suffer because of globalization and
cuts to services. You will suffer because capitalism is becoming more hard core'.
The gap between the working and the not working, rich and poor was about to
become widened. And the youth could sense that feeling of isolation from an
uncaring political society. So, they invented thier own world. Punk, post punk

cultures like early new romantics like Bowie and Roxy Music fans. Then came at the end of the seventies the main culture out of this era. The Casuals. But for the casuals to grow then needed food, and football and music was that food.

One more factor that made us angry was probably the sense of insecurity there was in the world. The fact that Russia and America were always at one another's throats has never gone away really. However back then, it was actually quite scary. The fear of nuclear war was so intense and that fear was later put into music by Franky goes to Hollywood with two tribes.

So we have insecurities, a feeling of isolation from adults, our own none publicized culture such as casual culture. We have political insecurity with right and left always in fighting. We have automation of jobs and globalization which causes employment insecurity. We had an unsafe society with fighting every weekend in all the pubs. Local gangs fighting one another for fun. It's a good job we didn't have hard drugs back then, the whole of the UK would have been anarchy and chaos. But really it already was. But we loved it, it was our era, and it was special.

In The 1970's The world was different. Not just a little bit different, it was dramatically different. The things people did day to day. Tasks like work, involved making things, and not sitting at desks. There was less pointlessness about things. Things mattered, and so did people, everyone.

But it's hard to look back and think how we filled our time without constant screens demanding our attention. How did we fill out that time. I'll tell you what we did, we met each other. YES, it's an amazing concept, how strange that should have been, meeting different people every day, without a reason to, just going to see them and talk, face to face.

These concepts today are probably quite foreign, and seem quite pointless. I can just imagine an 18 year old now saying, or rather typing "Shall we meet up erm, just to see each other". Reply by text generated by friend "What for, why do you want to see me, I'm here aren't I, tell me here now".

It was what pubs were for. Buy a drink, it helps you relax, talk about whatever comes into your mind. Relax and enjoy just conversing and receiving feedback to your every comment without feeling guilty about leaving a smiley or a thumb's up. What a dilemma that is, worrying about emoji's. Is this what we have come to? A trivia obsessed overweight population, who forgets about important things that are happening in far flung places. Will these third world countries desire to advance into a first world state like us. Will they see us as countries that they inspire them, to become like us?

This is the story of a time when things were more simplistic, and a little less complicated. Life was a little slower with less distractions, but it did have consequences, teenagers got bored and started to look to violence for entertainment.

And reality TV, what is that? The answer is simple really, it's the entertainment business trying to cure our appetite to relate to people, to become part of something and have a life. But this comes at a financial cost, but it didn't used to. It is now just a one-way thing, you watch them, and see them living their lives instead of living your own.

In the seventies, we took them risks, we called people names because it would provoke a reaction. We enjoyed that risk, and that reaction. Today everything is risk assessed, so if involves a risk, this would mean we would need to make a risk based decision, instead of having any risks taken out of the equation.

Does the youth of today want to live in a real world. What monster has our generation created? In a world where everybody sits in front of big silver screens, when the world outside is still turning and streets are deserted of life. Without actual interaction, where is action, the real action not the simulated screen action. No wonder half the kids are too fat, they don't know real action. The world has become False, it is already on the way to becoming a simulation. How many people do you see not paying attention to the real world now. They walk with their eyes elsewhere, on some little digital world that they carry around with them. The youth will take over this world and they will have known nothing else. Oh! For us to find a time machine and throw this generation into the seventies, how long would they last before they screamed that somebody called them a name that wasn't allowed, and cried about being told off by GOD FORBID a teacher.

Like what Irvine Welsh wrote "Choose Life", but they won't be able to, if they don't know what it actually consists of.

So we did risky things, and what happens when you do something risky like going on a rollercoaster. You enjoy yourself. If you got into a fight in the seventies with another kid, you had to make quick decisions, you had to learn lessons quickly. Today some kids don't even like facing risks as it gives them 'bad vibes', so they avoid risks, as this is what a politically correct society is telling them to do. It is us the parents fault too, we are not void of blame. We have been taken in by a safer society, we should know better, but time makes things fade away. Ironically life was probably more colourful in the world of black and white TV, well my mother's curtains were.

We now live in a world of fear. If you were ever to read Big Brother, which for some reason has now been popularized as a reality program. If there was ever an indicator that the powers that be were trying to hide something important, reinventing the meaning of that title would be the biggest culprit. So, if we did read Big Brother, then the world was ruled by fear. The country that we were friends with would suddenly change, to confuse us. How many times has ISIS changed its name.

Anyway, back to the seventies and how different it was. This story follows the lives of four teenagers, and how they lived their lives to the full, during the decade of laughs and fights.

The boys were trying out a new rope swing, Baz had to climb up a tree which was 40 foot up, but he was a scrawny git. His mum didn't have much money, so he didn't eat as much as he should of. It just made him really fast at running though, and climbing was easy with his long fingers and black pumps, that were supposed to be for PE in school.

There was a stream at the bottom of the rope swing, so if you timed it wrong your shoes would get soaked, or worse still you would get covered in mud and thump to the bottom, onto the stony bottom of the stream.

There was a rusted old fence, some big lads had ripped out some bars, and probably started hitting each other with them for a laugh.

This was the main road, and you could probably expect a car to come past every 30 seconds to a minute depending on the time of day.

There was seven dogs in the street. Mr Brady on the corner had a massive Alsatian that nobody had ever seen let outside. It was probably too screwed up, and would bite anyone and everyone who came near it, unless they were in the

Brady family. The dog was used to being locked up, as every dog was. Dogs were either locked up or roaming the streets. The dogs that roamed were generally quite safe, but if you had a cat then it was a different story.

These days' cats are well safe from dogs, because every dog is on a lead, not so back then.

Digger was a medium sized mongrel. Most dogs were mongrels, as having a pedigree was for middle classes or dog enthusiasts. Digger used to go into anybody's house, when he felt the need. He did get fed a lot and one or two times he would simply stay in another house, without any questions being asked.

Probably about 90 percent of people left their back doors open, and 80 percent their front doors. I think at night time these were always usually locked, as there were a few house robbers about at night.

Everyone knew everyone in the street and parents would often talk in their gardens over fences or privets, which were very common, as they were cheap to own and very easy to maintain.

Most people would sit out in their front gardens in the summer, and talk to pensioners who walked past. People always looked after the elderly, and kept an eye out for them. Mr Morris would often go to see if Mrs Jackson, who was in her eighties was alright. They would bring her some milk and sugar. Often the kids in the street would have a duty to go and knock at some elderly person's house and ask if they needed any shopping.

The kids would often get 5p or 10p to spend for going. John and Paul down the road often made some extra money for the holidays by collecting lemonade bottles and taking them back to the corner shop for a deposit.

"Being a new teenager is going to be really scary, I wanna do a Peter Pan and not really grow up". Gio was a philosophical kid who was scared of change.

"Think of the things we can do though Gio, like fire an air pistol. Set off fireworks, earn our own money".

Rod was a year younger, but just as wise as the other kids in this area.

These kids grew up to be hooligans, simply because they wanted to be. It was their choice, it seemed like all of their more daring mates went the same way, the ones with balls.

And a few years later in 84 they were back in that cold old station.

A trip to Scotland meant an early start. There were about 30 lads up in the concourse this day, and it was 5 in the morning. Two lads had been out all night and just decided to carry on to the match. One lad was called Oinker, as his brother was a bizzy, he never lived down this name. He just accepted his name, probably because he was overweight too. The word was Celtic had cavemen fans, like tanked up wool backs. They were usually up for a fight after a few drinks, but they hadn't yet embraced the casual culture, unlike Aberdeen and even Hibs.

The train journey was a long one, and there was only one toilet, which had a massive queue of lads the entire time. It was just like British Rail to forget about the Liverpool to Edinburgh train. Liverpool were playing a friendly with Celtic on a Saturday night, which was going to be chaos as the Road End boys decided to go to Hibs first to see what action they could find. Apparently, Hibs were had the start of a decent crew. They had taken some notes from playing Aberdeen, who basically took their style from the Scousers in the late seventies. There was a bit of grief between Liverpool and Aberdeen, as the scousers had stormed the place but didn't expect it all their own way at Hibs. The City Centre was massive, and the lads found the famous castle. They were supposed to pay to go in, but just jumped the barrier. Now what the scousers did next might surprise a few people, but it happened. The whole 30 of them started singing "Engerland...Engerland...Engerland". This only happened to wind up the locals but the soldiers posted outside the castle were not too happy and tried to clear them on. "Ger, yer orrible English arse outta this place, this is sacred to Scotland". The squaddies got a big boo, and some lads even pretended to charge them to provoke a reaction. A few of the soldiers jumped as there was only two on each gate, but the scousers soon cleared off after claiming their national victory over this castle. Back outside the Hibs ground, there was a few hairy moments. At one stage there was 20 Hibs onto 30 reds, but he Hibs were just interested in what they were wearing, and they got talking, and all shared a drink. A few of the lads weren't happy about the friendly approach, but a great plan was hatched to join up and attack the Celtic later that night.

So the two mobs joined up and caught the train at 5 to Glasgow. The celtic mob were not renowned for violence, or casual culture, but they did have a big fighting crew of the older variety. Yes, it was the bovver boys again, and a few skin heads thrown in for good measure. Some of these cavemen style had Birmingham bags on and a few still had long locks.

The mob of 50 joint up boys had to separate into gangs of five each. They even bought some green and white scarves. A few of the scousers still have these scarves today, so it was money well spent. The whole crew now managed to join together in one pub. Now Scotland has lots of pubs, especially Glasgow where there used to be a pub on every corner. So, each pub was used like a fortress. The mob needed to play a game of conquer the pub. The first pub was full of scarfers, but that is where the problem started, nobody knew if a scarfer was a scarfer, or a hooligan. So, the lads used this as an excuse to simply attack everyone. The first pub got gutted and there was Celtic running everywhere, they all retreated to the next pub. But the Hibs and Scousers started to take the next pub with not too much resistance, but every pub they took now would be more clued up as to what was going to happen next. In the fifth pub they started to meet resistance. There must have been 100 Celtic inside and they were very angry. The boys threw a brick through the window then stormed the place. As they ran in there was a wall of tables on their side, and behind them were tooled up scott's, who lashed glasses straight at them. The joint mob had to halt and retreated outside. There was no way they were getting past that table barrier. The next minute, what seemed like the whole of the pub stormed out at once. The battle started and it was bloody. If you could imagine, brave heart mixed with lord of the rings (well that's what Celtic looked like), then that was the scene. There were a few cuts and bruises, but the police arrived and had never seen violence like this unless it was an old firm match.

The scousers never went back to Celtic for years, but a few friendships were formed with Hibs, who would go on to become Scotland's best casuals.

9

Giro heist

The only form of wages some lads saw in the 80's was a little green cheque that came through the letterbox every other Thursday. This cheque became a source of happiness and lager for the lads, so much so that they wondered how they could acquire more of these lovely things. Some lads decided to have multiple names and go down to London. They would move around to different districts and acquire different names on different sign on days. So, the lads decided to break into the local Royal Mail sorting office on a Sunday when they knew nobody was working.

Remo even had a balaclava on for some reason, as even then CCTV was used here and there, probably more so in the sorting office where the staff could identify possible cheques.

The four lads climbed over a concrete wall, then smashed an outside window into the office. The security guard was asleep, they made sure of this the week prior. He always fell asleep between 2am and 6am, it was his little work treat. Around them were multiple sorting machines all switched off and piles of letters. They all sat down and switched on their torches. Remo still had his balaclava on. The place smelled of glue and mouse droppings, it was filthy with bits of Sellotape and spare elastic bands all over the dusty concrete floor. Rod had an Irish cousin and started to sing a daft song which left the lads stunned.

"A prudent thief should never drink so much that he becomes bold.
Because a thief who boasts and brags will rarely live to grow old.
For silence is a thief's best bet and if he breaks this etiquette.
Undoubtedly what he will get...will be more trouble than gold.

Consider Zhele a thief from Greel, who drank at the Swan and Grouse.
He made himself quite popular by buying rounds for the house.
One night in drunken revelry, he made a bet with prideful glee,
But later on he would agree...he never should've been soused.

A thief's best friends are luck and speed, alertness, cunning and stealth.
And ale can cause these all to flee and cheat a thief of his wealth.

But add to this a drunken dare to steal a lock of the Empress' hair,
Then even a fool should be aware...this may be bad for your health.So Zhele did
stumble through the door in his most fearless state.
He slipped in shadows past the guard and snuck through the palace gate.
Then giggling he scaled the wall so drunk he thought he could not fall.
For wasn't he the best of all...and surely favoured by Fate.

As he climbed in he saw a girl who was dressed in cloth not fur.
A palace maid? Perhaps a cook? T'was difficult to be sure.
A homely lass she did appear, but anyone looks good through beer,
So when she asked, "Why are you here?"...he said he was there for her.

He showered her with compliments for flattery was his skill.
And so they spent a pleasant time as any young couple will.
But as the dawn lit their embrace, he recognized the lady's face
From every golden coin it graced...and suddenly he felt ill.

He'd heard that drink was dangerous and now he knew for a fact.
For thieves caught in the palace were hanged or stretched upon a rack.
But as this thief was kind and bold, the empress gifted him with gold.
(Then the guard made sure that he'd been told...he'd be killed if he ever came
back.)

And so he was a thief no more for that was part of the deal.
His bet was lost because she gave him what he went there to steal.
So other thieves may scorn and mock his name and tale but still they flock
For a drink and a look at the Empresses Lock... the finest tavern in Greel."

The lads all gave him a clap. "Fuck Rod, how did you remember all them lyrics"?
Gio was fascinated by music.
"Me dad used to get drunk with me uncle, they would drink whisky for hours
then start singing 'ye drunk, ye drunk you silly old fool', dead funny like. I
prepared this song in case we got bored".
The lads then told each other to be quiet as they might wake up sleeping beauty
in the next room up the corridor. The giro letters were quite easy to identify, as
they were brown and had the queen's logo through the envelope square hole.

They were racking up quite a few, then they got bored.

Rod opened other letters and the ones that looked like personal ones seemed to be the most entertaining.

Rod stated laughing listen to this lads, what have you done John. "I love you dearly but I can't carry on like this John. You never bring me anything nice, and often stay in the pub til late without me. I'm leaving you tonight and I'm taking Jake the dog, because he loves me more than you, he always sleeps on my side of the bed".

John looked over, "Well your John as well Rod, that's your fist name isn't it? I'll find a better one."

John scurried through loads of letters and Remo complained that he should be looking for the Giro's but John wanted to find something better.

"Eee are, get a load of this "I'm sorry I missed you yesterday, it was because I've had a change of heart and I don't want to see you anymore. It has always been complicated with me. I was always confused about boys. You must understand, it's just not you, it's me, I'm different than other girls. Last Friday I went to town and there was a bunch of girls, some sort of youth Womens institute movement, we all got along so well. I was drunk and I got carried away, there was this girl there called Julie. She showed me what it was to be a woman, she took me home and we gave each other such a wonderful time. It's something that you could never do. John I'm like a book now, I've turned and your history. Sorry Sal. X x"

Remo and Gio were laughing too loud and the guard seemed to make a noise. "Fuck you all, be quiet." Rod didn't laugh at the reply as he knew it was a bit better. He stuffed a load of personal letters in his pocket. "Shit, them poor lads will never know why their girlfriends won't answer the phone no more, this should be a national pastime. Fuck up some one's life in five easy steps, It's an occupation mate, with a red top. People actually get payed for doing this" Nobody laughed as there was another noise. Remo looked up and felt the low wooden roof. "It's fucking rabbits running across the roof".

Everyone relaxed that's when Gio found a little present. He had walked next door and found a room full of parcels. "Fuck lads, it's Christmas, let's get into these instead". Remo wasn't happy as he was getting plenty of giro's. "Why don't we just carry on opening the giro's lads? Your never gonna get that stuff over the wall". Gio disagreed "I dunno feel a bit guilty about denying scousers their giro's, they'll be fuckin riots around here". Gio carried on scurrying around the next room then entered the room with three bottles of Jack Daniels. "It's not Christmas lads, but its new year's eve, let's get stuck in."

Remo was getting a bit narked now "After that song Rod was singing, didn't you listen to the fuckin words. Basically, it said 'don't get pissed while robbing' you'll all end up waking up here with police dogs around ye". Nobody took no notice and they all started on the JD's. Rod even pulled out a double sized rizla and built up a big spliff to share.

After two hours of searching, they heard a police siren head up the road. Everybody stopped what they were doing, and John woke up and dropped the empty bottle of JD onto the floor, it smashed with a rather loud bang. Then they really did her the Guard move in his chair. Rod threw his still lit ciggie onto the floor and looked panicked. All four lads had their pockets stuffed with Giro's and head stuffed with pot smoke and JD stumbled up and headed for the corridor. The Guards room was down the corridor, but the exit door was the other end. They didn't bother being quiet, they couldn't in their state. Then the torch was on and it pointed out of the doorway at the bottom. "Hey, who is that, is it you Tracy have you brought me some cake again." The lads giggled and Rod shouted "Not tonight Josephine". All four lads tumbled out of the door and athletically got over the wall, except John who was still half asleep, it took him three goes to get up and the guard was on his tail. He grabbed Johns foot, but john did a lovely back heal into his chin. The lads looked around for any bizzy cars then ran through the quiet morning back to their estate, through all the back roads and over school fields so as not to be seen.

The next morning it was on the local radio news "there has been a fire at the local post office, many letters and cheques were burned, a guard has lost his job as he was seen to be unable to guard a room only 30 yards from his, where the fire started, foul play is suspected. There was murder down the dole which was besieged by people demanding a new cheque. Gio's girlfriend was one of the ones effected, he didn't know of course until he came to cash it, which he did with the help of his sister. He got the extra money and she got a replacement anyway.

10

Huyton Invaded

During one quiet afternoon in 84 a big cheeky gang of Chelsea decided to get off in Gods Country. Yes! They actually tried to invade one of Liverpool's toughest districts without letting anybody know their plans. If they would have let us known, then we could have had a welcome party waiting for them. I would love to hear their side of this story one day, if some cockney ever wants to fill me in on what they think happened, it might be enlightening.

Anyway, back to the story. They decided to stop early and have a bit of fun in my home town, talk about taking liberties. There is a pub right outside the station exit called 'The Queens'. Chelsea just waltzed in. There was about 70 boys.

"Alright gov'ner, pint each for all the lads, how is your fine town, any scallies about this good day". It was one of the Chelsea big wigs who lead the little expedition. Now, Huyton is not really a wealthy town. The best thing we produced was a cracking addition to Liverpool's mob, a few biscuit factories, Steven Gerrard (a few years later), Freddie Star (best not say no more about him) and The Huyton Baddies. The baddies were a decent crew who had organised the DSS Tour to Mexico during the world cup. A couple of the older fellers used to follow the reds in the 60's and knew exactly what this was.

"Aye lads, What's with the big crew this time of day, down here of all places? Have you come to kick off with Knowsley United"?

"Where are your hard boys? Is this a tough area or what old man, all I see here is relics from the sixties and crumbling concrete". The big cockney was not impressed and spat on the floor as a sign of disrespect for this damned place.

The old man looked around, "Nothing doing here mate, we're here for a quiet pint, have you tried the St Johns Estate, or Woolfall Heath. They'de batter you cockneys around there."

"Fack your wool estate geezer, just get me someone to kick off with otherwise I'll smash your town centre to bits and scare all the little old scouse ladies."

Another cockney chipped in "Yes and we'll eat all your pets while we're at it."

The cockneys started to sing Chelsea songs at the top of their voices, and refused to pay for any ale.

What they didn't know that Huyton was full of scallies, and they had been seen at the station. Now an invasion of Huyton was not going to go down with the locals. A lot of the locals never even attended any games but liked a good fight, especially of a Friday and Saturday night, usually among themselves. But there was a special treat in town. Huyton is no small place and is packed full of council house estates, where working class is the order of the day. Five lads were waiting for the train to go east and so where waiting in the big yellow train shelter. These lads followed the blues, never did the away matches but loved the last 20 minutes where they would storm into Goodison and kick off with anybody and everybody.

"Fuckin cockneys, in our town, the cheeky bastards. Let's get the Bluebell Estate up, Pagey and Longview. Jonno, you get to Mosscroft, the Bakeys and The Johns. I'm going straight to the Quiet Man, The Eagle and down Woolfall. Let's teach these cunts not to come to land on our turf.

The whole 4 of them looked comical as they stooped down only the eyes and wedge heads were visible in the shelter. As they left the shelter and down the subway they carried on stooping and looked like monkeys on a mission.

After 25 minutes of drinking the Chelsea were getting itchy for a fight. So they turned right under the subway, and headed for the town centre. As they entered the dark and vandalised subway, all they could see was "Fuck Man U", "Jimmy Kelly murderers ","Road End Boys ","EFC","LFC","Huyton Bads " and "I shagged Mary D ", all over the subway walls. They never felt intimidated and started singing the Jams "Down the tube station at midnight" and "Run, run where ever you may be, we are the famous CFC, We'll run you all, wherever you may be, we are the famous CFC".

As they walked towards the concrete mess we called a town centre, they first walked past the job Centre, the first bastion of scallies. A few windows went straight through and they started to sing to the tune of you'll never walk alone. "You'll never get a job". Ten lads ran out, some still had pens. Then another twenty ran out of the betting shop and started shouting abuse. But the sheer mass of cockneys was too big for a confrontation, and Chelsea knew this. They still had a little go at the small gangs. Next to join the affray was twenty lads from the Rose and Crown put. They cautiously walked towards the Village. So, it was already up to 40 against the hardcore 70 but they were badly split up. Half of the lads from the Rose still had works uniforms on, probably out for a dinner time bevvy, the other half were just men in their 30's and 40's having a nice weekend drink before hitting Liverpool Town Centre later that night.

Chelsea surged into the town Centre and ran straight into WH Smiths kicking all the books and magazines over and scaring the shoppers, around the next corner and they stormed into the only sports shop in the town which was ironically called "Pride and Joy". A few were drunk already and put all sorts of track suits over their current clothes. Chelsea didn't know they had been collared getting off the train and it was only a matter of time before the local estate mobs landed. There was a sweet shop which was pilfered and a cake shop which they stormed into and grabbed what they could. One fat Chelsea lad had cream all around his gob.

The council Estates were emptying of their lads and it wasn't far to march to the village. They picked up wood, bottles, bricks and anything else they could find on the way. Some lads even grabbed plant pots out of people's gardens. Out of the other estates came 40 to 50 lads each. Which made a mob of 250. Now probably about a quarter of these were boys from the match. But everyone knew what Chelsea wanted and they were getting it. Chelsea did have one lad go back to the station in case it got too much on top. From the North, South, East and West came Huyton's finest. This was going to be some welcome. Chelsea were still pounding shops in the Village when half of Huyton arrived. It was an awesome sight, they simply charged at Chelsea who stood for a while as there were some good hardcore within this crew. They stood for about 3 minutes waiting for some sort of police presence, which did arrive eventually but not until the locals had broken a few noses, ribs and regained some pride in this fine town. Never again would the cockneys invade this overspill town. The police regained order and formed a chain guard around them until the train to town arrived.

11

The mods scooter trips

A local town called Southport was one of the main daytrip for many lads and lasses from Liverpool. A few of the casual fans had joined a little scooter club who called themselves the Liverpool Mods. There was a slight change in the clothes. Instead of track suit tops, jeans and trainers. They simply changed the trainers for tan brown Rockport boots, and green or navy fury hooded parkas, with band names on such as The Specials, The who, Madness and The Jam. This little gang had some fun in the resort especially when they went looking for rival rockers and mancs. This one day both John and Gio had bought lovely new shiny Vespa's fresh from some Italian dock. Nobody knew why they were so cheap, but you could buy anything from the back of the Eagle and Child in Page Moss. Gio was not really into the 60's stuff but liked madness and The Jam, actually everybody liked them. John was wearing his Specials black and white t-shirt and Gio had his Rolling Stones tongue top on. Gio had strapped a ghetto blaster to the back of his bike and had his own tunes banging out, this was a thing a lot of the scallies would copy in the future. Madness was the first playlist, Gio actually stopped to turn the tape over. Everybody laughed at him when he gave his reason for stopping and told him to buy an auto turner type player, but he couldn't afford a sony Walkman, just some crap from Rumbellows shop. The Jam was loud as fuck all the way around Southport promenade. The boys were all buzzing, then it was time for ice cream and chips. There is a place where the scooter and biker crews stop near the start of the pier. This is where they came a cropper.

These lads thought they were all so hard, then just eat ice cream and chips, what a travesty to violence.

As they were sitting there eating Ice Cream John recognised a few boys from the match. Fergo and Lanny were hanging around and they got talking. It appeared that there was a big battle planned on the beach between the mancs and scousers. As the lads were being entertained my local break dancers and body poppers Gio changed his music to grand master flash. A lot of the mods didn't like this and there was almost a fight about it, some lads actually drove off in a huff, but Gio wasn't a music snob and liked a bit of everything. Some mod was calling it plastic music with no substance. Gio quickly shoved him away and gave him that nasty stare. Gio was trying his hardest to convince the mod gang to confront the mancs, but some weren't too happy as they weren't hard-core violence fans at all. Don't get me wrong they had been in a few scrapes but the football violence was probably another level. In the end half of the scooter club decided to go down to the prom to see what the all the fuss was about.

When they got there a few football lads waved at them, and a few looked at them suspiciously as there had been some fighting between mods and casuals in other towns, but nothing yet on Merseyside, after all scousers just didn't fight amongst themselves, not in the 80's, maybe in the noughties but not before.

Fergo walked over "Where's ye proper gear lad? What's with the big stuffy coats"?

"It's just a style thing lad, we're running with the mods, while the footy seasons over".

One of the mods, started up his engine and black smoke started to puff towards Fergo, John kicked his bike "These are our mates, don't be a knob Jacko."

Fergo just smiled and moved a little away from the smoke.

"What's the deal Fergo, you got any smoke bombs, or did you get any flashbangs off that lad in the marines again. They really put the shits up them bouncers that day in New Brighton."

"I've got a few fireworks and bits and bobs, some reckon the mancs are tooled up, so we've got a few bricks and metal sticks hidden in the sand".

It appeared that the scousers had robbed loads of those stripy wind breaks from the local shops and had lined them all up in a row, so the mancs wouldn't see them hiding behind.

Fergo had a new arsenal up his sleeve on this day. He got the idea when crossing his school field as a kid. Some looney had one of those air guns with sights on and was shooting him from a distance of about 300 yards. He had armed two more lads with sighted air guns and twenty other boys had air guns, which shot multiple shots, but had loaded them with tiny darts. These were not accurate guns but them little darts really stuck in you and they knew they would cause panic.

The mancs started arriving bit by bit. The first crew walked over to the scooter lads and started asking them if they had seen any football lads from Liverpool. Gio and John had said they heard something might happen so they came down to watch. The mancs were not friendly at all, one lads was booted off his bike, he quickly gave a scowl and got back on. Two other mancs started letting tyres down and soon as the numbers were better on the scouse side, the scooter boys all jumped off and chased them over the sand hills, and kicked fuck out of a few. But the scooter boys knew that a big mob would be here soon, so they found some concrete seaside shelters and hid in these with their bikes still parked up on the prom road. Some scooter boys kept their helmets on just in case some nutter manc had heavy weapons.

As the day progressed Fergo realised they were getting outnumbered, but the mancs still hadn't found them. There was about 30 windbreakers and the 3 lads with sniper guns had dug themselves in, they had got carried away and build what only could be described as makeshift bunkers. The mancs now numbered about 50. There was 20 scooter boys and 30 football boys hidden away. Fergo knew this was now the time for some fun and they started to sporadically shoot down their sites at the mancs. It looked really funny at first, it was almost like they were trying to shoo flies as bullets flew around their heads. Some lad got hit in the arse and was jumping around like a bee had stung him up the arse. All the mancs were confused and started to duck down. One knob head even tried to hide behind a six-inch pole. The mancs were dressed just like scousers as they were into the gear very early as well. After initial fear of what was going on the mancs got more confident and some held up shields made out of dustbin lids quickly robbed from local hotels. As they marched forward towards the sea, and the direction of the pellets, the fight started. About 50 yards from the wind breakers which were all red and white for some reason, the scousers stood up and gave them ten rounds of dart pellets. This was the funniest site of the day, as almost all of them were hit and the darts were going right through their clothes, they were almost performing an African co-ordinated dance not unlike the break-dancers earlier. The scousers were laughing their bollocks off, and started to advance. The mancs backed off a few hundred metres as they pulled the little darts out of their skin. Some lad even had one between his eyes and was hesitating about going back. The little kids who were helping them out came back with more bin lids and the fight was then on, as numbers were now on the mancs side, or so they thought. The mancs advanced again but this time they used bin lids as shields and they advanced slowly and almost had a Viking shield. Fergo hadn't expected this but he had one more little trick up his sleeve. As the first wave of attackers approached 25 yards from the windbreakers, with stones and bricks launched they got a bit cockey and didn't expect any more tricks. But the ground collapsed from under them and twenty mancs collapsed into a ditch. "Plan two" some scouser shouted and fireworks fired towards the three ditches that were prepared. Aerial bombs exploded and some poor mancs ears were ruined for a few days. A red smoke bomb was thrown into the pit, and the scousers charged. The mancs managed to scramble from their two-foot pit and the scousers again fired pellet darts. The mancs were disorientated and retreated to the promenade. The scousers were now at a disadvantage having fired all their darts, but they pulled up their hidden sticks and bricks and had another go.

The mancs now had the high ground and weapons of their own. They still had numerical advantage or so they thought. From the back of the prom the scooter boys attacked their rear as the mancs attacked the steps where the scousers were attempting to clamber up, fully armed to the teeth.

The scooter boys fully helmeted charged at the rear and the mancs were flanked. The scooter boys had a great go, and looked awesome and scary with their helmets and mod gear. Two lads had old style bovver boots on and laying into the mancs good and proper. Bodies went down and the Road End boys clambered up the steps. This was too much for the mancs who charged up the street back towards Southport station. There were loud cheers as the joint scousers cheered to defeat their main foe on this sunny bank holiday Monday, what a great result it was for them, and their unconventional tactics and newly gained friends gave each other hugs and laughed their nuts off for hours. The usual spliffs came out, and the lads started planning for the next bank holiday. A few of the scallies even got rides home, even without a helmet, they knew how to live in the fast lane anyway.

12

Red and blue make a purple patch

All the City derbies around the county are massive events that seem to entice vicious rivalries that last for decades. The only derby that was truly friendly was the Merseyside derby. Red and blue always mixed to give the scousers a purple patch amongst the countries violent outbreaks. The Road end boys used to go to Goodison Park every weekend when they weren't going away. That steep, steep stand was the cause of some vertigo among the unfamiliar reds. Gio and John were perched on the edge one day, and a bit of a scuffle ensued. The red lads wouldn't go near it, because if you looked down there was a forty foot drop to some convenient barbed wire fencing. Just one nasty punch and you would be down, cradled by the spikey wires, and swinging liked a spiked medieval soldier.

So the reds and blues used to mix and swell their numbers at away and home matches. The grounds are so close and are conveniently perched in a battle park conveniently called Stanley Park, I wonder who thought that one up.

It was December in 83 and Everton were playing Aston Villa. Now the Villa were a handy little crew and like all big cities, they had quickly latched onto the Casual culture thing. Villa had a big crew, as the city is really only second to London in size, so there was a lot of unemployed and pissed off youth ready to vent their anger at everyone and anyone. Most of the country hated scousers, probably something to do with jealousy of Liverpool and Everton's success in the 80's. The city really did dominate the football hall of fame. It would be Liverpool's season to win in 83 by just sneaking by (believe it or not) Southampton but Everton would eclipse Liverpool the year later to lift the most coveted crown.

But the Everton crew and the Road Enders would all mix, they were basically all from the same schools, and pubs and workplaces. They had a comradery that nobody else could have as they were the most oppressed city, so they had one common enemy, the whole of the country. Although secretly there was an affection for Glasgow, Newcastle and Dublin who had similar outlooks on life. This is probably where the chant "We're not English we are scouse" originates, from the Celtic and Gallic roots of this fine city. If you looked deeper, you would see that the city of Manchester was probably the closest in demographics, unemployment, outlook and poverty. But nobody would ever admit that secretly they were our closest cousins with so much in common it was unreal. This day a lot of Villa boys decided to come up to the Pool on coaches. There are only so many coach parks in and around the ground. Quite a lot of Everton's boys would hang out on County Road, which is a busy road quite close to Goodison. The road spanned for a mile North and on virtually every corner was a pub.

There is another pub quite close to the ground called The Oak, I was also a resident DJ there, but he landlord got angry when I played YNWA one night. In the old era it would have just been laughed off, but in the noughties, this was extremely naughty and I wasn't there for long.

Anyway on with the story, of how Liverpool and Everton fell out. It actually took a fair few years, and the main culprit was obviously the ousting of English teams from Europe, but the seeds were sown a lot nearer to home, and Aston Villa played a part.

Remo, Rod, Gio and John were on the prowl in County Road for Villa, they were joined up with a few of Everton's boys called Phillo, Brains (named after someone from thunderbirds) and Barra. These were also from Huyton and Remo didn't get on with some of them because of an earlier barney between housing estates.

This day the boys were all divided up all over the place, as in the 80's there was distinct lack of organisation by all clubs. West Ham were probably the only organised gang in this era. It seemed that this day The Villa were a bit in groups of eight or ten at first as well.

The word on the street is that some Villa had gone up to the Glebe which is a fair walk. The argument started between the blues and the reds about how far they should walk before they could get their next pint. It started to get silly for the sake of 500 yards, so every stormed into The Brick. The Everton crew were all massed around three tables and gave the Liverpool lads a funny look. It may be that a few thought that they may have been Villa themselves as it was starting to become harder to distinguish between crews. At the end of the 70's only Liverpool really dressed like they do, with a few Everton copying the blueprint. The Liverpool lads all had Ellesse bucket hats on which was the latest trend and they did look rather dapper. The blue's kept trying to pull them off and then chucked them to each other. It was a childish and almost school like prank, and the reds fans simply ignored the antics, which sort of spoiled their joke. There was always going to be divisions but they were very light between the fans, obviously on match days things were a bit heated and banter became intense.

Remo was on form today "There is a depressed Liverpool fan in the bogs, he's tried to hang himself".

Rod was toking on another spliff "Your fuckin' joking, what happened".

Remo smiled and said "He was turning blue so I cut the cunt down".

Rod didn't get it and looked confused, then sniggered to himself.

That started them off and Gio was next "Why are all blues smelly, …. So blind people can laugh at them too".

A few blues gave him the finger. And come back with "what do you call 5 reds in row touching ears, a wind tunnel". John returned with "What's the difference between a fat bird and Latchford….The fat bird at least scores now and again". It was all friendly banter and a good laugh really. But time was running out and needed to look for some Villa. They walked outside and it was trying to rain. Even though It was Warm three of the lads had bubble coats on, which was ok if you got slung against a wall but not to cool down with. Then they heard the brummie voices, and it was time for fun and games. Five brummie casuals walked past and gave the boys daggers, one was wolfing down a hot dog, almost like it was the last one he was ever going to get. They got ten yards up the road then started gesturing for the scousers to come and get it. One lad had a police telescopic truncheon. All the lads steamed in and two Everton lads got lashed with the truncheon before they wrestled it off the Villa lad, who was surprised it was gone, and clueless how to fight without it. They took turns to lash him with it over the noggin. Remo was in a full blown kicking match with two lads, who seemed to know all of his kung fu moves and how to counter them, it started to look like a Bruce Lee rehearsal.

Rod started swinging his arms about trying to catch them unawares, he still had a spliff and smoke and sparks were flying everywhere. He took one full in the stomach and went down like a shot Jap during the war.

Gio and John were having their own tussles but turned around and stopped Rod from getting stamped on, they were always good like that looking out for one another in trouble. A few more Everton started piling out of the Brick pub, and it was time for the Villa to be on their toes. They got chased right up County Road, but there was about ten keeping a low profile in the next pub which is called the Chepstow Castle. The ten Villa stormed out with pint glasses, there was only a few Everton scarfers in there but they walked out to see what the trouble was. The two small crews joined up, but by this time the mixed crew of reds and blues where well on their heels in pursuit. Load of pint glasses and bottles rained down on the scousers and it brought them to a halt. They all stormed into the Chepstow castle and the blue scarfers ran out to get out of the way. The red lads wanted the Villa to know it wasn't just Everton chasing them, as Everton seemed to get more credit for violence than the reds. "Liverpool, Liverpool, Liverpool". It sounded more like a war cry "Everton, Everton, Everton", was the next chant. The brummies must have bottled it because the whole of the city was out to get them. Three windows went through and the Villa tried their hardest to barricade the door with two round tables. But it was bound to go through any minute, and so it did. Sirens sounded as the landlord must have quickly phoned the cops so his boozer wasn't smashed up to fuck. As the scousers invaded they faced them off against the bar, half of them jumped over the bar and started to lob full bottles of whiskey at them, but it only held them back for a minute. Then a Villa lad was hoisted by his two arms and legs and thrown right through a window, he landed on his back to a nasty bone cracking noise, and the fans outside just laughed. "That'll teach you to provoke the scouse hoards lad." Rod simply couldn't help but put the boot in with that comment. Then the only window that was intact also became a human smash zone as a smaller Villa came through trainers first, and somehow landed on his feet and simply carried on running down the street away from the mayhem. Rod and John looked at him and felt like clapping for his aerobic talents. "Fucking seven points to the Villa for that gymnastic trick, they've got

more than Everton already", Gio was also impressed.
The police arrived and everybody scattered, they ran after a few and one blue was nabbed and thrown in the back of the maria van, for his fun and games.

The word got around that there were three more Villa coaches arriving, and that they would park down on Piney Avenue. So, the lads decided to group together both Blue and Red and try to storm the coaches. The only way to remain inconspicuous though was to split up and get there through the back way, which meant traveling through Anfield cemetery and re-joining together again. As the joint crew of about 40 reached Pinehurst they were in luck. The Villa supporters were just arriving and two coaches were full of boys. So, the scousers would be outnumbered but more where on the way. As soon as the buses stopped bricks were thrown and about seven of the windows went through. Some Villa didn't even bother getting out the door, as the back windows were massive. About ten piled out and another 20 from the front, and the fight started. The joint force of scousers has stolen vases from the graveyard, and quite a few got thrown straight at the Villa. The few Villa that got through ended up with vases smashed over their heads and they quickly retreated back to the doors. There was 30 Villa onto 30 scousers, and nobody was winning, although the Villa were pushed against their bus. You could see the rest of the boys egging each other on to go outside, but some wouldn't budge, they had lost their bottle. The second coach load who were not casuals seemed to want to join in, and thirty half-hearted fighters tentatively ran towards the scousers who started throwing what was left of the vases. Three big older fellers who have must have been old skin heads had no fear and stormed into the crew. Three scousers each grabbed them and started kicking they all over the floor like a football. One man realised he had bitten off more than he could chew and started to scream like a woman. It did work though as the lads laid off him, in case he alerted the police, not unlike a rape alarm device. Now the third coach started to let out after a few bricks were thrown. The scousers were well outnumbered now, but the two factions of scousers seemed to split up into red and blue. The Villa started to give chase, this was embarrassing and the result of not being organised again. But a few of the Everton had a plan which they didn't notify the Liverpool fans about. The blues waved their red friends to follow them, so they did back towards the grave yard. Villa were now in full pursuit about 60 boys and 30 scarfers and up for it old skinheads. The Villa were quite fresh as it was only two hours to drink up the motorway. They started to gain on the scousers. That's when the decision was made. The Liverpool lads all shouted 'stand' and stand they did, but the blueboy's decided to carry on running back to the graveyard for some reason. Remo, Rod, Boiler, Gio, John, Julien, Jaffa, Doyley, Fergo and a load of hangers on were not relenting on home soil. They got some great digs in and fought as hard as they could under the circumstances. Rod had already got a lump of concrete over his head and was bleeding quite bad. John had two black eyes ready for tomorrow, Remo had a cut head from taking that many face punches, Gio was fighting his best but had lost a shoe and had a busted-up face, it was time to retreat or go to hospital. The Villa didn't expect such resistance from such small numbers and seemed to let them depart out of respect for their stance. Not that Villa usually showed such guile and comrade for their fellow casuals but this time they almost applauded the scousers stance. The Road End boys followed their traitorous blue friends into the graveyard. As they entered Everton jumped out ready for a raid, but then noticed it was the reds.

"Where the fuck did you'se lot run to? We were getting twatted down on Piney". Fergo was not happy that his top was ruined with claret.

"Waiting for you to follow us, wankers, it's a raid, we needed to lead them here".

"Well why didn't you tell us? for god's sake!" Fergo looked furious and so were the other lads.

The top blue boy walked over and smacked Fergo in the face, a single man fight started, and Fergo was already injured. Everybody broke it up and the Everton boys re-iterated the need to hide and wait for the Brums.

Then they appeared the whole sixty of them, and from nearly every grave stone the blues charged, and this time it was all out war. The reds did help them begrudgingly. It was one massive ruckus and lasted for about five minutes. There were about 20 bodies lying on the floor from both sides when the police arrived who were no doubt informed of the fight from local residence who backed onto the graveyard.

About half an hour later the Road End boys turned up in the Oak pub on Walton Road, and funny looks were given from both sides after the little altercation. The tension you could cut with a knife, then a pint glass was thrown at the Road Enders and all hell broke loose. This was another nasty clash and probably the first one since the 1960's between the supposedly friendly rivals. The police were quickly called and dealt with the disorder with nasty truncheons from both sides. All Liverpool fans were then subsequently banned from The Oak for another twenty years before a certain DJ played YNWA.

13

Spurs Away

Twelve of the lads were up on the roof area again, on Lime Street concourse. The morning was nice, and everybody had come early again, nobody had a Friday night drink this time, as the last trip was a disaster due to hangover horrors, for most of the lads. One lad had turned 18 and it was a big night. They had started off on home brew that somebody's dad had made, and it was a bit rough. The sun poked through the concrete doorway and Rod was being daft again. He bought a packet of king sized Rizla's and tried to weld together three long ones. It was drooping at the end, and tobacco and black Morrocan was leaking out the end. He lit it up and took a big drag. "Fuuuuuuuuck, that's good". A few of the lads saw him building up and they had formed a little queue. Gio was next in line as soon as he took a drag he realised this roll was far too lose and it burned his throat, but wow was this strong. Gio, staggered backwards and actually slid down the wall onto his arse. "Yeeeeeees, that was decent lad, what a way to spend a lovely Saturday morning." Remo barged Jaffa out the way and grabbed it off Jaffa who was in the middle of a drag. Jaffa's eyes lit up and he gave out a sigh. Remo was in a mad mood again and took about 3 drags without breathing in. He started to go white and forgot to breathe. He simply looked outside towards the sun and it changed colours. The doorway looked like a rainbow entrance and his knees trembled. "Fuckin' heaven, I see it." He unconsciously murmured and everybody heard it. John instantly snatched it out of his hands and had his own drag. Remo was still in his dream and didn't even notice it was gone, he eventually started breathing and had a sit on the concrete for a bit. John had a drag and the end fell off, it had a baby spliff and one became two. The lads were there that long that they simply missed the train. Seven of the lads walked down to Mount Pleasant (yes, a real place) and hired a transit for the trip. One of the older lads called Dug had a driving license, the other lot hid around the corner while he hired it, they had all clubbed together and it was the crews first trip via the roads down to Tottenham.

They hit the M6 and noticed some cavemen in coaches, it may have been Blackburn or Man U fans who were travelling South. A few of the lads had put down their tracky tops as them wheel arches were so uncomfortable. Fergo and Remo were in the front with the driver, who they told to keep doing sharp brakes and fast turns. Gio, Rod and John were shouting to "Fuckin pack it in, were getting wellied with bruises in here." At one stage, somebody unlocked the door and Gio started throwing bits of rubbish and empty cans at the traffic behind. Everybody needed a piss as they were starting on cans of Harp lager. The first service station was one near to Stoke. A few of those Man U and Blackburn seemed to have the same toiletry needs. Stoke were travelling North to Everton and nobody knew who was who. The lads all poured out and a blanket of pot smoke popped out as the door was opened. Everybody had red eyes, even the driver. Off to the service station they went. There was a bit of security about to stop too much robbery during these heady days of summer. The lads simply looked at the man in his fifties with distain as if he could stop them lot. Straight to the café and bog. Everybody grabbed a pie or pasty a few cakes, some lads even paid for a bit, as they wanted to get to the match before any trouble. At the back of the restaurant was another gang who had been travelling in a similar van. They looked like a bunch of vagabonds too, one lad even had the cheek to wear some colours, it was Stoke. The scousers immediately ran over, and asked for a go. The Stokies looked confused that somebody would so openly and quickly challenge them, as this really was a hard-core crew. Two of them waved Stanley knives in the air, and it was time for a quick exit. The scousers kicked things over to stop the pursuit, and Rod grabbed a bread stick on the way out, as if it would be any use but it was the only thing he could find. The security man was hollering into his radio as the scousers ran past him, Remo slammed the door on the stoke, and the lads grabbed stones on their way back to the van. They started launching them at

Stoke, who were still in pursuit. The van started up as the driver seen what was happening and the lads jumped in. The van headed straight at the Stoke nutters who jumped out the way then started throwing bricks at the scousers. The thuds alerted the scousers to the attack. But they escaped without a single cut. "I know what I'm taking next season at Stoke" Gio said to John who agreed revenge was due to them twats.

They carried on down the M6 and all needed a good piss again. The driver was getting a bit fed up stopping all the time, and probably was a bit pissed off because he couldn't drink. Then the little songs started and they kicked the back door open. Now it wasn't normal songs, it was songs about places that sounded stupid. To the sound of 'here we go' they sang "Staleybridge, staleybridge, staleybridge, pontefract, pontefract, Pontefract". As the van slowed down Jaffa got booted a few times, and started screaming as he slid out the door and onto the road, there was a robin reliant behind and its one wheel nearly went over his head. He jumped out of the way, then gave the fibre glass gimp car a kick in the door. There was a man who looked like Mister Bean staring at his through this Guinness bottle glasses, but he decided to carry on because fibre glass cars don't dint, they either break or don't. The car was hit with such force that it wobbled at the front and Jaffa was scratching his sore arse and giving the lads the 'V' sign.

Gio thought of a suddenly 'dad joke' and said "we should buy a robin, cuz that's all we ever do". There was groans and somebody threw an empty can at Gio's head. He waved his wedge cut as if it was fuck all to him. To the tune of 'Go West' they sang "Jaffa's fell out again, jaffa's fell out again, Jaffa's fell out again".

They stopped at Wolverhampton services and they charged to the toilets, John kicked a bin on the way in and lots of rubbish showered over a scruffy old man, who just looked on in distain. "Young bloody hooligans!" he shouted. "And proud of it", John shouted back. The sound of "Scousers here, scousers there, scousers every fuckin' where", echoed in the foyer. But they didn't realise that again they were being watched, but this time it was Wolverhampton who liked to lie in wait for visitors to their service station. As the scousers left the bogs, they heard this deep throaty chant. "Yam, Yam, Yam, Yams". There was about 30 of them and again the scousers were well outnumbered. Some of the lads had orange tops on, they must have been the scarfers who had joined up with the yamyam boys of Wolves. This time there was no knives, so the scousers decided to steam in, mad that they were. Remo and Fergo charged at the brums. They didn't expect it and all the scarfers scattered, this put the Yam boys on edge who backed off a bit. Remo hit one full in the face, and he stooped down without falling. Fergo's boot caught another boy in the stomach, he looked quite winded and bend doubled over as Fergo targeted some lad in a blue and white benneton top. "Fuck brummies". Johns turn to charge in, and the 15 yam yams who were left were on the back foot, they didn't expect seven lads to go at them so hard. John and Gio charged in and landed some blows, the Yam yams had had enough and scarpered back to their hide out, where ever that was. The road end boys chased them outside and the brums jumped over privets, one lad seemed to land in a bunch of nettles. The scousers ran towards their van knowing that they would be fucked if the big crew got their senses back and retaliated. The back doors were still open and they all jumped in in unison banging bodies. For a laugh Remo shouted "Drive driver, anywhere, just get the hell out of this concrete shithole." The lads laughed and they all agreed to have a go at the yams again next time they hit the M6.

"Jingle bells, jingle bells, jingle all the way, oh what fun it is to see, Liverpool win away ho." Gio was singing on his own, and got a slap from Fergo. "Give it a rest Gio, its only fuckin' February."

The next service station they needed the loo again, and it was around Coventry way, it seemed that these young lads had a pissing problem, I wonder why? John and Gio were wary of Coventry as they had a big battle there quite recently, but they all needed a piss and to rob some scran for the journey.

As they got out Fergo played his ace hand and put on his mask.

"What the fuck is that? Freddy Crugar." Rod was puzzled

Fergo had a welding mask on, a thick welding coverall with a massive Fila sign painted on the front of it. "Where are Coventry, Where are Coventry, Where are Coventry". The boys copied the YamYam type of chant to seek out their foes, Gio looked a big sheepish and didn't really sing anything. As they got inside they ran down a snack isle and started to pilfer the sweets and crisps. Remo had a few ciggies in his front pocket on his Peter Storm cagool. As they left the toilets they were all a little bit hungry. There was a self-service counter and they served themselves then shiftily walked away to two sets of plastic tables. They all piled through the pies, gravy and chips. John had too many stolen pies without gravy and started to lob them at Jaffa, Rod and Fergo. Fergo caught one plumb on the noggin and was calling John everything under the sun, when some couple started complaining to the kitchen staff about food everywhere. A lady who looked like she was on minimum wage (and that was all she was ever getting) came over and tried to complain. She got another pie straight at her ample bosoms. She just started crying and walked away. John was laughing his bollocks off and the mood changed to 'let's have a laugh'. The mood changed again when a line of casuals walked straight in, and there wasn't just a few of them it was a coach load of Bolton casuals.

"Let's do them, lets fuck them off with pies." John was in a mischievous mood and lobbed the first pie. The lads all ran over to the food and the kitchen staff just backed off. Gio grabbed a bowl of hot gravy and the lads all ran over. The Bolton casuals stood and started moving towards the scousers. "The Road End, the Road End." The boys all shouted as they launched the food. Gio was feeling brave and waited until they charged at him. He then launched the hot gravy at three who were wearing white and yellow tacchinni gear. He knew they would be ruined. "Bolton, Bolton, come on scouse", they shouted together like a rabid mob ready to kill. The lads were all young, and managed to scarper away as quick as possible. These were proper boys and no scarfers this time. As Rod left he slammed the glass door. Gio was not prepared for this and simply stuck his foot out and the door instantly smashed to pieces, Gio was scanning his body as he charged through the bits of shattered glass, he felt just like his hero as a kid, the incredible hulk. The van was waiting again, the driver expecting another chase and they all charged into the back, Gio was patting down his Lutah ski jacket and looking for any cuts which strangely there wasn't.

"Fucking 'ell Gio, you're an animal, how did you do that lad."

"Dunno, Ive got strong legs, I think."

"Gio (Geoff) kapes lives again", John was laughing and Rod felt guilty for accidently shutting the door.

"Sorry Gio, I just automatically reacted, didn't realise you was behind me."

"It's alright lad, with no reaction there is no action, Jackson".

A few bricks hit the van again, and they were off to London for a day with the fans who called themselves 'the yids'.

It seems Fergo had organised another little surprise for opposition fans. He was still in the front with the driver and Remo. He had made sure the lads hired this sort of van as it had a massive sunroof, which was lift-able to form a larger roof capacity, almost a concertina construction. The lads stopped again for another piss, but this time it was at the red lane, and they all did one in the bushes. Fergo got the lads to life the concertina roof off and stored it in their limited sitting space. Rod jumped into the top and lit up another spliff. By this time a lot of the lads were half cut and were in a mood to do anything for a laugh. So, they waited for three coaches they knew were coming down the motorway. They had spotted them full of Man U scarfers and a few scalls. They waited on the motorway embankment and as the first bus approached, they got ready with the paint bombs. Fergo had filled twenty balloons full of red paint. Four bombs went arched straight at the windows. The coach slowed instantly and the windows all opened. Out popped loads of manc heads a few of them had red paints splashed. "Ye fuckin twats, who are ye, who are ye. "Bastards, we'll have you." Three of them jumped off the coach as it stopped and started walking down the red lane towards the lads. All 7 of them charged, and three had more paint bombs. As they got closer, the mancs seen what they had in their hands and retreated back into the coach. A load of abuse was shouted each way and the scousers started up their van, and started on part 2 of their plan. The coach was still stationary as they went past. The ugly faces that the mancs pulled sort of stunned the lads. Whether somebody had let some of the muppet's free or somebody purposefully told them to mug a face nobody knew, but they were ugly enough to cause a bit of repulsion. "Fucking hell, they're so ugly, when your mums dropped them off at school, she got a fine for littering". Rod commented. "Them mancs are so ugly, It's the reason animals eat their young." Remo opened another can and the van slowed down, now doing 50 in the slow lane waiting for their next victim. A police car turned up, and everybody returned to their normal seats and tried to look inconspicuous. It blasted past about 90 probably to the next service station, then the five lads stood on the missing roof section and waited for their next victim, which didn't take too long. A big black coach, it said Salford coaches so it could just be another set of mancs. As soon as it started to overtake, Fergo shouted "Lads, wait until its right in the middle of us. Let's see what their faces change to when we attack the bastards." Every lad launched a paint bomb at once and there were a few open windows. The bus slightly lurched towards the van, and the Bernie had to slow right down so it did not hit them. Smoke billowed from the tyres and you could see the alarm on the faces of the travelling fans. A big cheer went up from the scousers van. The mancs ran to the back to see who the fuck had attacked them. The coach decided to carry on as a matter of safety so the scousers did a "motorway pirate" and overtook them. The van and coach were now both travelling at 60mph and the scousers got a good look at the mancs. Jaffa had his Liverpool hat on so they all knew who had attacked. There was a mighty roar as the mancs shouted everything at once. Some big feller was scowling and shaking his fists. "Scouse bastards, we'll kill you" somebody shouted out of the window. Fergo caught him full in the face with a paint bomb and everybody saw him jump back alarmed by his red face. Some manc pulled his pants down and mooned the scousers, a very sorry sight, a middle-aged fat arse. A few more paint bombs were launched and the coach eventually slowed down then stopped.

"Ok lads, the pigs will be looking for us now, I'm using the A roads now, there's only forty odd miles to London.

14

Lost in the Forest

The lads met up in Stanley Park, sitting on the swings, and climbing on the climbing frames. They just sat there waiting for something to happen.

It was 10.30 am and all the matches always started at three, unless it was a European match or a cup match, which were usually night matches. There was about 15 in the crew today, and they had already turned up waiting around for a possible rival gang. The team today were Nottingham Forest, who had become a big foe for the reds. They had been one of Liverpool's biggest rivals on the pitch so that naturally transferred to off the pitch. Remo had bought a new pair of sunglasses, which were slim line and modern looking; he looked almost like a skier. Remo had long curly hair, not unlike Kevin Keegan, but nobody ever slated him about it, it was just who he was and part of his mad attire. Remo and Rod had semi-flares on as these had just started doing the rounds. The jeans were Lios and Lee. Rod had a lovely pair of Adidas Jeans on, and Remo kept saying he may get them taxed down a dark alleyway, either that or the suede will get really dirty in their first fight. Remo was probably jealous as he only had a pair of Adidas Trim Trab. These were all the rage but the problem was Gio, John and all the rest of the lads seemed to all wear them as well.

"You's Huyton lot all look the same, has the local sports shop gone through or something".

"Yeh, we did the golf shop, drove a golf Kart through the window, they didn't even have alarms. Me and John fell asleep in there as we were already a bit bevvied. The grass cutting man rudely woke us up, doing his early morning duties, fuckin liberties."

"What have ye got?"

"Le Cost t-shirts, any colour you want fifteen quid."

Just then, three lads walked around the corner with curious accents. They sounded a bit like wooly-backs but a bit posher, with a pinch of brum. They looked straight at the scousers and were on their guilty heals.

Remo looked at them and just shook his head. "Three of them, not worth pounding my fists for, let them go, we will get the snots later."

"They'll bring a load back them Forest bastards, should have rendered them useless." Rod wasn't too happy and was ready to chase them.

In the end five lads decided to follow them just to see where their early mob was hiding out. The fifteen of them then decided to hide out and wait for any Forest who would return. Fergo's idea was to wait near the duck pond. There was paddle boats all tied up, quite close to Goodison Park, it was a place where boys lit up their spliffs and enjoyed the peace and quiet before the violence ensued. All thirteen of the lads ducked down while Julien and Jaffa went looking to entice Forest towards the pond.

Rod was not happy "I cant believe you've left thirteen of us here, it's a bad omen. Either these boats will sink, the ducks will turn into something out of a Hitchcock film or Forest will be fifty strong. Gio looked over. "Go to the Arkiles and get some re-enforcements Rod, some of the boys hang round up that way, get yoggie or boiler to join us. Rod was happy to leg it up the hill just in case, his beige Burrbury flapping away. Remo lit a spliff up and started to relax in his boat. "Fuuuuuck this is the life" then he started to sing 'row the boat'. Fergo untied his boat and he started to float off into the middle of the pond, but he really didn't notice as he was fully lying down now, head in the clouds in more way than one. Rod came running back in a panic and jumped straight into the nearest boat. He couldn't get his words out fast enough "Fifty of them, chasing Jaffa and Julien, they were doing fucking zigzags trying to not get battered, they're coming this way. I did alert a few of the lads and they said they'd be down in five". You could hear them coming, it was like charge of the light brigade. Julien and Jaffa simply followed their instinct and dived straight into the water. Julien squealed like a big girl as he realised the water was freezing and his nearest change of clothes was in Letchfield. The forest where in no mood to take prisoners but they weren't getting their clothes ruined for the sake of two scousers. Everyone waited with baited breath.

One of the forest lad's looked over curiously "What the fuck is that boat doing on its own, with smoke coming from it?" Remo heard the ruckus and thought the lads were fucking about, he pulled his body up and instantly saw he was 30 yards out to pond-sea and 50 angry forest staring at this ghostly figure waking from a dream. He simply used his instinct looked at them and calmly said "You want a drag or what you a bunch of benders, whatever floats your boat." Julien and Jaffa waded over in the mud and grabbed the spliff off Remo then had a drag each. Jaffa looked at the all in the eyes "Come on in lads, the waters lovely". The sheer cheek of them mad the forest even more furious but nobody wanted to get covered in mud in their expensive gear. Then there was a few murmurs about a crew approaching. It was boiler and yoggie with a crew of 30 lads. Forest ran straight towards them expecting their superior numbers to win the day. That's when the hidden pirates jumped out and flanked them. Rod, John and Gio kicked them all in the back. Yoggie, Boiler and his crew ferociously attacked from the front. A few lads had cricket bats and knocked out about two forest who were now in a panic. One forest lad had lost two front teeth, and blood poured from his gob. Rod couldn't help but laugh at him and shouted "You need to get into farming lad". The fight lasted about five minutes; it was ended when the three creatures from the black lagoon started throwing mud bombs at forest who didn't want mucky clobber all day. So they simply legged it over the hill towards the police escort.

As the crew walked back towards the stadium, Julien and Jaffa went to a local house for a shower and ended up with some curious clobber on.

15

Scally music

Everybody loves music especially teenagers. That's why duringa a hot sunny dayo Gio, Fergo and a few more lads decided to form a rock band. Now whether that band was ever going to be successful nobody knows, but some people say that they started an era of music called Britpop. How did this happen, well everybody copies the best. The La's copied the The Road End. The Stone Roses and the Happy Mondays copied the La's and Oasis copied their respective Manchester bands. But the lads who actually called their band The Road End after their other part time hobby following the reds on the terraces. The influence of the The Road End was Simon and Art Garfunkel, Pink Floyd, The Who, The Jam, Madness, The Specials, and the Small Faces.

Gio was absolutely skint so him and john used to go down to the St Johns precinct shopping area and steal sports gear to order. He ended up making close to £900 to fund his band. Their attire was basically just terrace gear. The concept they wanted to convey is that you don't need to look like a knob to be in a band, you could just be the local scally down the street. They toyed with the idea of calling the band "The Scallies", but they were worried that venues wouldn't let them play if they attracted the wrong sort of clientele. It even ended up with the group playing in one of Liverpool's most famous pubs, where the Beatles played before the The Road End followed in big footsteps but couldn't really ever reach that high. You can still download three songs by The Road End on Spotify to this very day. Judge yourself whether they started the big British Rock and Roll revolution or where they just pretenders.

George a decent feller, no much of a casual but the band members made him wear the gear which he wasn't really happy about because this stuff was expensive.

Gio loved the music, and thought he was a cross between a mod and a scally, he loved any type of music, but mellow rock appealed the most. The slow Rolling stones stuff, Paul Simon, folk from the seventies and Pink Floyd. The Floyd stuff went together with the smoking ganga, and the culture started to be called Retro Scally. The two-tone stuff greatly influenced the kids at the start of the eighties, madness and the specials where the specialists, and everybody loved them and vandalised their school desks with their motifs.

Fergo was already an excellent bass player and was a lover of Joy Divisions bass riffs. He based all of his lead riffs on Joy Division. He loved to play and would do it for nothing, but it was proving to be quite profitable until....well I will get to that at the end.

Gio was a decent singer, but he had taught himself keyboard too as he also liked the electronic music of the eighties.

The last member of the band was well this is hard to say these days but his name was Richard and sometimes liked to be called "Dick" and he lived up to his reputation sometimes, he was basically insane. He went to college with Gio and ended up throwing bits of spark plug at car windows every day. The windows would instantly smash and the lads would give it toes home.

They used to practice in the St Aidens church hall, the manager there was called Barney, he was a bit of a tyrant and actually charged them a tenner a go, even if the lights were off.

Their first gig was at a notorious pub called the Huyton Park. After much practice, they were starting to sound like a new type of band, a fusion between sixties drug rock and seventies folk/soft rock. This sound was fused with a bit of synth from Gio, that gave it an eighties edge. Fergo had actually heard a bit of Frankie knuckles disco house and had asked Gio to try to include some within the music. Dick was not happy with his drumming being superseded by a machine, but he went along with it as him and Geo got along very well. Gio liked

the fact that Dick had no idea of shame and would do anything to shock.
When they got to the pub, some kids asked whether they wanted "Either their vans minded or their windscreens blinded". "What the fuck to you mean kid" Fergo looked at him like he was a piece of shit ready to be rubbed off his shoe. "Well, you'll find out if you don't give us fifty p mate". The lads all knew what it was like around here so thought it would be safer to pay the kids, after all they probably would stop anyone doing anything for half a quid.

As they set up, about thirty lads arrived. They were requests all night "You got any ska lads, any specials, do some madness, do some rolling stones". All the lads wanted to do was to play their own stuff and make people aware of their style of music and how it could change things, 'a new fusion of rock and sixties psychedelic', is what the advert said.

As the night progressed, a few glasses were thrown at Fergo on the bass. Fergo walked over to the thrower and threatened him with a 'bunch of boys from the match'. "Fuck off lad, it wasn't even me, you come round here and expect us all to like your tuneless crap, just play some Stones."

In the end the lads played some popular stuff, it was just the safest thing to do. Dick found the same lad at the end of the night and twatted him over the back of the head with a microphone. It was Gio's favourite mic as well, what a waste. I've still got the deformed SM58 to this day. The lad's mates came around and tried to get at the band. The little kids actually started throwing stones at the big lads, who couldn't get close enough to trash the van. "Fuck Huyton off lads, let's go to Woolton or somewhere next time, I paid loads for this bass, and the sound system wasn't cheap". A few weeks later Fergo went up to the St Johns estate and had a bit of a riot with the locals looking for the perpetrators. He later found out that a couple of the lads followed Everton, that leads to the blues and reds chapter and how the resentment between the two sets of fans started. It never existed until this point.

The next gig they had was going against everything that they had decided and was again in Huyton, this time it was around the corner from their practice venue in The Quiet Man pub. If ever a pub had an opposite name to what it actually was this was the place. It was all the lad's local, so they presumed they wouldn't get any shit this time, they were the rulers around here, but the problem was people heard that they were good, and came from every estate on

Huyton. Where a load of bad boys congregate you always get a load of fit girls. The 'in' girls always want to be seen with the bad boys, I think even Wham admitted this then proceeded to dance like pansies.

The lads started off with D-trains "You're the one for me". Nobody knew what it was so Gio sang over it with delicate psychedelic harmonies, it sounded great. They never did it again and it was the only every time they did it, it's a pity it wasn't recorded. The gig was going well until the request for the usual request for Peter Gabriel, Genesis, Pink Floyd. The lads eventually played a few as a stool was slung at them, when they played a few of their own numbers, which to be fair were a bit rough around the edges. The girls were swooning around the group at the end of the night, as they knew it wouldn't be cancelled as it was their estate. Dick had actually smashed through one of his drums when they finished with Anarchy in the UK.

The band actually left their gear down in the cellar as a precaution and they all walked home pissed. Before they walked back they were sitting on the wall outside the car park talking.

"What's the point in doing this, if they just throw shit at us", Dick was rightfully confused.

"Well the point is, to show the authorities, the judges, the teachers, the politicians, the tories, thatcher, the police and anybody else who tries to suppress who we are, exactly what we are, and what we stand for" Gio was being philosophical again.

"But what do we stand for? Why will they take any notice?" Dick was still confused as he started lobbing stones at taxis who flew past at 1am.

Gio sighed "We need to show them what we are made of, we need to be heard. We can't always be those working-class lads who all work on the building or become house painters."

"They won't listen to us, they don't need to, they have the money, all we've got is attitude."

"Maybe, but I've got a funny feeling they want to be like us, to have balls, to have guile and a need to rebel against something. I reckon in the future everybody will try to act working class, because it will be seen as cool. In thirty years time, they will use our words, our slang and copy our music. They're just all backwards looking. We can see the depth, because we have been at the bottom, we can see how high we can go. They have already been up there and don't know what it's like down here."

"Fuck, Gio, you've got a great way of looking at things. I reckon you should make a song with them lyrics. That was brilliant lad."

Gio looked at Dick and was still in a philosophical mood "Good idea lad, a bit like that dignity song by deacon blue."

The next gig was as a support act in a club called Eric's in Mathew Street, nobody knew how they managed to get on the bill, but it was probably a link Remo had to the bouncers down there, he was always mixing with shady types. So, they got a place to project what they were, and it was full of football and trendy types, the people who actually set the styles. There was talk that New Order and OMD where there that day, but the lads never got to mix with them and had to get changed in the toilets. That's what happens when your first on the bill, and last in people's minds. That is starting off though and the things you must do to try to make it in the business.

Gio was even driving the van, and had to find somewhere out of the way so nobody smashed his windows, as there was a combined tape, CD and radio player installed.

As they waited for the doors to open to take their gear in the manager opened the doors and looked at the lads with indifference and no interest. "Set up over there, you'll have to take it down yourselves too, no help here lads, oh and don't trip my switches".

The night started and people where coming in quick. It was a real popular venue and the lads started to feel a little bit nervous. This really was their ultimate night and they couldn't get nothing wrong. There were a few decent local bands watching too, that they probably ended up influencing, such was the music business. Groups tried to latch on to trends and make the trend their own.

They started off by playing "What we're made of" then "Violence for the masses" and then "terrace culture". These are the songs you can still find on Spotify, by The Road End. They seemed to go down well, but the three songs on where all they were allowed to play. In effect, they had another seven sorted which was enough for an album. But this album never got produced and will go down in the dusts of time of 'what could have been'. The songs are still in my possession which I will probably release one day as a complete album from the edges of time, (a good album name actually).

The girls again were very interested in all the lads, as they were really at the cutting edge of fashion, with their retro scally looks. These looks were copied much later by Oasis, the happy Mondays and the Stone Roses. They wore wax jackets buttoned up to their necks, each one had adidas Trim Trab on and Lois boot cut semi-flared jeans. Dick had a pair of black Kickers on, and they all had wedge haircuts.

George almost single headedly peeled off two girls and looked a bit shocked at the attention. The others were all wallowing in it.

The next gig knocked them back down to earth, it was in the St Aidens Club and they were playing to an aged audience who kept asking for Elvis. This was becoming hopeless, they really needed a decent gig. So, it was off to Manchester and it was a risk they knew. Some of them might be known to the Manchester hooligans as there had been so many battles over time. Gio in particular was scared of being recognised, as a Man U manc was slashed and he saw it, and almost got some blame.

It was the 02 Apollo, quite a nice venue, but the area was as rough as Kirkby's arse. It was proper shady and the boys were all on edge. There were eight bands on that night and The Road End were again only allowed to play three numbers. It was so close to an area where Gio and Fergo had had a massive run in with the Moss Side loonies and Man City's crew. There was a couple of old Punk bands on as well, and headlining the night would be slaughter and the dogs, trying to make another comeback.

Fergo and Gio were terrified as there was some real scally types mixed with the skinheads, rude boys and punks. As soon as it was announced that they were from Liverpool there was a muted boo. The punks came right to the front and started to spit at George the drummer. He was not best pleased and it soon started to hang from his nose. Fergo stopped playing and ran over to two of them and smashed them in the face. Gio realised a riot was about to occur and decided to give Fergo a hand. Then it really did break out, and a few casuals came to the front and instead of attacking the scousers they kicked off on the punks and gave their fellow casuals another ten minutes to play their stuff. This was the biggest surprise of the night as there were a few known United and City firms in that room. There must have been some sort of recognition for fellow hooligans, and there were simply no hooly bands about at that time. Dick wanted another kick off though and was still cursing "Them dick head punks" during the trip home.

Our records got better and better though. I was the main songwriter and the beats got funky and psychedelic. We got a bit of a small following in Liverpool only.

There was arguments about transport and commitment but mostly about why we weren't earning no money for our efforts.

The last gig we did was at The Jackoranda which was another old Beatles haunt. The gig went great, it was probably our greatest gig and we had about 30 fans turn up. We did the whole album, and it was like birth of a 1980's Pink Floyd, but it all went downhill when we failed to get paid by the gangsters running the place at the time. It was the End for The Road End, and we simply fell back into hooliganism as a remedy to our rock blues.

16

West Ham away again

LIVERPOOL FOOTBALL CLUB

LIVERPOOL
VERSUS
West Ham United
24th NOVEMBER, 1981

MAIN STAND

Ticket & Match Information
051 260 9999 (24 hour service)

ROW	SEAT No.
Nº 17	123

MATCH SPONSORED BY:
Radio City
This Portion to be Retained

The Road End boys were the first scally / casual mob and West Ham were soon to know about it. Five of the older lads had decided to be more organised for once and had five cars. Remo, Rod and Fergo were in with Doyley. Gio, John and Yoggie were in with a lad called Morris. The cars were all old, some on their last legs but the lads were just proud that they were using a modern means of transport, rather than the rickety old trains. "You up for this one today lads" Doyley was all decked out in new gear, nobody knew where this lad got his wedge from but he always had a few pennies whenever it was necessary. "We're up for it, how does it work though. I reckon we could get caught out if these cars get separated". "Nah, this car's fast enough, we just need to keep up with the joy riders ahead ". Rod started to light up another spliff, this time it had a red tip. "What the fuck is that?" Remo was confused. "It's a retro scally LFC rizla, that I got made for me and the lads". "Who the fuck made them? Giz a look" Remo snatched the customised rizla's. Each paper was extra-large in size and had the emblem "Road End boys on the Riz" embezzled at the top of each one. At the very top it had three red stripes and the adidas sign. "Fuck Rod, these are class, did somebody print them specifically for you?"

"Yeh mate, they're made of special paper too, it has hemp mixed into the paper to give that specific black Moroccan smell." It so happened that the cars pretty much stuck together and seemed to want to do 110mph all the way. Although Doyleys car could only do 80 he was left behind a little. There were no mobiles so people had to just wait around for one another or arrange to talk from specific phone boxes.

Everybody was impressed but Rod informed everybody he was getting some Johnnies the same treatment. Now they felt like royalty.

A few warm cans of Harp were bandied about. Remo had eaten a curry last night and remnant arse air was leaking from his trousers. One stink bomb was that bad that they had to pull over on the red lane. "Fuck Remo what did you eat a dead horse or something?" Fergo was having a real go. "I reckon it's this cheap lager, it's shit we need to buy some expensive foreign stuff, like San Miguel or Breaker." The boys carried on but really couldn't catch the others up in this Ford Granada, it was like a tank. "This car fucking stinks Doyley, what's up with it?" Rod was looking at the floor for some holes.

"Yeh, there's just a few holes, about that, it's just a few fumes and apparently it was used in a farm for a while, there was something nesting in the innards and he did mention that they drove it into manure one day, cuz they thought it was a shit car".

Remo started looking under the mats and using crisp packets to block up the holes so weren't fumigated.

"Fuck! Doyley, all my ganga smoke is escaping, what a waste." Rod was laughing.

That's when the smoke from the exhaust stated getting worse.

"Jaysus Rod, how much are you smoking back there? Have you seen our contrail".

"It's alright, it's probably because I'm using red diesel". Doyley looked pleased with himself.

"What you mean, blag petrol lad." Fergo was worried now.

"Nah, it works fine, I heard about it from my dad's mate. What you do is mix methionine with chip pan fat, and it works fine. It's the cheapest fuel I've ever bought. My auld fellas mate owns a chippy, got me tank filled for nothing".

"Is that why I can smell fish, or are we going past Grimsby again." Remo looked like he wanted to get on a bus all of a sudden.

The car was letting out masses of black smoke, and chugged a bit now and again, it was like a dying German bomber, ready to crash and burn.

"How we gonna find the boys Doyley? We're bound to be late now".

"They're gonna be in the Queens pub on Green street. If not, he has the local phone box number which I'll call."

"Should have got the train, at least they don't pollute you and leave you stranded".

Remo was still worried. As they reached the North Perimeter Road all the boys were buzzing simply because the car had reached London. The trouble was Rod was reading the map between piping on his spliff. It's a wonder he could see properly with all the smoke, not to mention the foggy head he had today. Rod was doing his best despite his obvious handicaps "Turn left at Northern Perimeter Road, then carry straight on until you see a butchers shop".

"A fucking butchers shop, there's loads of them things around by West Ham,

every other dad is a butcher. Where are you getting your directions from Rod".
"Er some cockney cunt I know wrote them down for me, he says he always comes down from Liverpool to see his parents, it's well the best way".

"Well, he may know where Barry the butchers is but I don't, I'm gonna have to follow the direction signs, that is the ones that haven't got vandalism written all over them like Mugswell Hill and all that".

As they were stopped at the lights Remo decided to have a bit of fun and shouted out at some cockneys "Who do you support lad?". He was ready to launch some CD's he had found behind the seat. "Liverpool mate, why who's asking". "Nah yer alright lad, you give me a good answer, We'll twat West Ham today, and beat them on the field too." The lad realised these were scousers and smiled and gave the thumbs up. "Fuckin' ell, haven't these lot got any good local sides to support, that fucked up my trick completely."

The next bus stop there was three white lads and two black lads all with baseball caps on. "Hey cockney, I've shagged yer sister last week." They all looked up and one of them said "It's ok mate, he's shagged his own sister too." The load of lads started laughing and Remo was disappointed again. Never-the-less he slung some classic CD's at them anyway, as nobody was responding to his taunts. One of the lads caught the CD and returned with "Fackin hell mate, that's shit, have you got Rick Astley as well and Wham." Remo took exception to the Wham jibe and was about to get out when the lights went. The door swung open and Remo half fell out. The lads laughed again and shouted "It's the fall guy".

"Let me know when you're about to pull off Doyley, I was just gonna twat them cheeky cockney bastards".

"Alright Remo, keep yer knickers on lad, plenty of time for that yet".

In the other car Gio and John were making great time, but the journey was anything but slow. They had been racing one another, and John even started to spill his lager as the cars weaved in and out of the traffic. At one stage the police had taken exception to the race, but simply couldn't keep up with the semi powerful cars. The police car was a Ford Cortina, and was quickly burned off and attacked with half empty cans of lager. At one stage Morris pulled up next to the police car at 80mph. He gave them the finger a crazy face and did a quick nudge towards them. The looks on their faces was a classic, like some sort of comedy cop out of Charlie Chaplin. They must have been from some sort of back-water county like Warwickshire as they didn't seem to have a clue. They slowed right down and stopped pursuing. The other four cars were all in line as they entered London, and they all parked up in Green Street and walked to the Queens with not too many problems. As they walked into the pub there was about ten cockneys, but the lads knew that they needed their full contingent, and waited around for the other five to arrive.

As they found a butchers shop they turned right towards central London. Doyley turner around and looked at the three lads.
"OK lads, we are small in numbers, as we walk from the car to the pub I have supplied everybody with a few little toys to repel our potential opponents".
"A fuckin' rotor blade, do ye think I'm gonna kill someone mate, not for me that one". Rod was quite surprised by the size of these weapons.
"How are we supposed to get past the thin blue lines with a baseball bat. What the fuck is this a golf ball with razors built in on string, bit lethal that mate".
"Well you never know with these West Ham nutters, you've got to fight fire with fire la".
The lads started driving down a street and fans were everywhere, but nobody had claret and blue on.
"What the fuck are Spurs doing here, thought we supposed to be seeing the ICF in action Doyley." Rod was confused again, as he supped on another spliff.
"Well it's your mates directions, you sure he wasn't a yid fan"?
Remo broke the conversation by throwing Dennis Russos CD's at all the spurs scarfers. Some lad gone one smack in the face and fell over. A few spurs started looking over. "Fuck off yids" Remo shouted. "Liiiiiiivvvvveeeerrrrpooooool".
"Fuck Remo keep quiet, we could get crowded in here and this isn't my car".
A few spurs walked over and looked at the car. "You scouse, stuck in this traffic jam, what's your game."
"Football lad, why what's yours fucking cludo, it looks like your clueless." Remo chucked another disk straight into his eyes.
A number of Spurs boys then ran over and kicked the car.
"What you'se scouse bastards even doing here?"

That's when Rod and Fergo jumped out. They looked like something out of a Bruce Lee film. Rod had a baseball bat and was swinging it around his head. "Come on cockneys bastards, have this", he swung at the nearest ones. A big bunch of spurs scarfers fell back, there was no boys in the area just yet, just have a go hero's." They quickly scarpered when Fergo started swing around the rotor blade. It started to get quite close to Rod who was still a bit dazed from smoking his draw. Rod jumped back into the car as the traffic lights had changed. Fergo was still swinging it as fast as he could and loads of people backed off. He had a job slowing it down without hitting himself. He jumped back in pleased with himself. "That was a brilliant weapon Doyley, but put yer fuckin' foot down, I think I've stirred up a bees nest. The Yid army are here. As the car sped off about twelve Spurs boys were shaking their arms asking for it. Rod navigated them back towards the East End and they arrived on Green Street and simply parked down a side street. "Let's leave them weapons in the car he lads, they were more trouble than they were worth". "Yeh our fists are hard enough" ,Remo said. "I don't know I'm into Chinese films at the moment, I brought these to practice on cockney nuggets". Doyley pulled out two num-chucks on a chain. "Yeeeeeeees get them down your kecks Doyley, just in case them ICF mugs pull us up". The lads tried to blend in, but still looked a bit too scally for the London lot. As they approached the Queens, they cautiously looked past the frosted windows, through a little bit of stained glass, that already looked broken. As they walked in they were greeted by a brilliant sight. The whole five carloads of boys were singing the Road End songs, and were quite pissed. John and Gio jumped up and hugged the lads. John looked excited "We've had West Ham trying to get in here three times, I think it was just their junior crew as they were a bit naive and expected us to run away and not throw glasses at them. Fucking wallies, We've been waiting for you'se lot to come in so we can go out raiding the cockneys".

Fergo pulled out his num-chucks and gave them a whirl, everybody cheered, then Gio walked over and gave the lads two pints each. "Your fucking late, did that shit wagon eventually make it Rod". "yeh only just though, Remo tried to get us killed when we took a diversion round White Heart Lane."

Fergo laughed and said "Nah, blame the navigator."

As soon as the lads had gulped their first amber nectar, a brick smashed through the window.

The brick was just wrapped with a piece of paper. On it was big letters saying "ICF get ready to be raided".

Next to come through the window was a banger. Everybody jumped then ran to the exit. The barman looked cagey as soon as he saw the brick.

Fergo still had hold of his num-chucks, so he lead the way and ran straight through the door. As soon as he ran out a tin of white paint smashed against his midriff. It looked like the juniors again but this time there was about 20 of them. So, the fight was more or less even. The cockney's were armed with paint and some clown had a feather pillow. What the fuck he was going to do with that was anybody's guess, but it probably involved some sort of strange attack after the paint. The cockneys must have known that the scousers all had expensive clothes on. Fergo was not happy as he swung around his num-chucks again and ran towards the juniors on his own. A few backed off. Now Fergo didn't really know how to use these things and managed to twat himself in the arm. That's when the juniors knew that it was all show. Fergo retreated feeling stupid and the two sets of fans clashed right in the middle of Green Street. The cheer went up for ICT even though they were not the proper ICF they were just playing on the name. But around the corner it was another story. There they were Cass Pennant, Bill Gardner and the rest. They were on their way to the Queens for a few before the match, and were also on the lookout for some scouse bastards to cut up. They heard the cheer and knew it could only be one thing. They were about 400 yards from the action and decided to leg it, even though the law were on their tail again.

Now the scousers were generally a bit older and stronger than their West Ham foe, but one cockney had a blade. Rod booted the blade straight out of his hand and the lad managed to cut his own wrists a little bit. He ran off, and so left the bravery of the junior crew. As they started to run they heard another roar from up the road. The crew ran to the end of the road and by this time the scousers could hear the roar too so decided to stop and wait to see who this was. When the junior crew caught sight of their saviours around the corner, the scousers twigged that this invasion was not friendly.

Remo shouted "The real ICF is here let's get to safety, run lads, towards the ground".

So the chase ensued, this looked kind of funny because 20 police were chasing 40 West Ham who were chasing 20 scousers, this was The Benny Hill show all over again. Nobody was giving any ground, except the coppers who were all a bit too fast to catch any of these youngsters. The horse brigade was notified of the trouble. The scousers were throwing anything and everything they could find at the ICF crew, who were now starting to gain on them, it seems that your legs weaken faster if you are in trouble. Luckily, the scousers ran straight into a convoy of fans who were being escorted to the ground by lines of police. The police caught up with the combined ICF and juniors, and the battle started between the police and the ICF. The ICF threw bin lids, cones and bricks at the police and this riled up the crew getting escorted. There were a few boys in the escort and the whole of the scousers were now ready to riot as well. They broke through the police cordon and charged at the West Ham who were busy smashing the police. The ICF were caught fully from behind and ten lads went sprawling to the floor. Pennant, Gardner and his boys then pushed on back at the scousers, but there was a lot of scousers, even with their combined might of the ICF they couldn't make inroads into the scouser hoards. Now a lot of these scousers were not scarfers at all, and the ICF was caught a little short on numbers on this day. It so happened that the police stopped a bit of a one way fight. The scousers were put back in their convoy and the riot was quelled. You've got to give it up for the ICF though, they were bruised but their pride was damaged and the followed the convoy all the way back to Upton Park trying their hardest for a battle. One lad got lashed into a police van for his persistence.

When the lads got into the ground, they went straight over to the away end. Rod and Remo had Fergo on a bet. They wanted to try to get into the away end one day. There seemed to be only one way to do this. The stewards always had a few spare vests in the crisis room, and Remo knew where this was. As the lads worked their way down they needed a blag to get through security. "Friends of the players, lads", Remo tried, "Grobbalar request extra gloves" Rod tried, but nothing was working. Fergo was more switched on and knew that the stewards were on low pay. "Three to pass" Fergo formally requested as he held a twenty pound note to the nearest steward. His eyes lit up and he showed them through. They went straight to the crisis room and picked up three orange vests.

They simply marched down the stairs opened the fence gate, got onto the pitch and walked down the pitch towards the away end. Fergo knew where the hardcore fans would wait so he avoided that particular pen and went into a scarfers pen. As soon as the three lads were in they threw their vests to the floor and started to lay into the nearest scarfer. The scarfers scattered, it made the lads feel invincible, they were taking on the whole end by themselves in their eyes. They knew they would quickly be apprehended, but the buzz of doing it was worth the effort. They also knew it was risky, as they could get surrounded and twatted at any minute. The roar went up from the away end and the three lads got a few jabs in before the police nabbed them. The main West Ham boys were about to intercept them, but they were that little bit too late. This is what situation the boys counted on happening. As they were marched back towards the police room, they waved to the crowd who all gave the loudest cheer of the day "Scouser aggro, scouser aggro". Remo managed to do a bow, and Rod lit up a spliff on the way, he was feeling completely cheeky. The coppers quickly took it off him and stamped on it. A few of the boys started to sing their names, as you would sing a player's name, even the normal fans joined in, and the three lads would become terrace legends that day, to rival Jaffa who got thrown down the kop at the end of every league winning campaign.

17

European Cup final 1984 - Roma

Sometimes you would simply like to do things your own way, but you just don't
have the money. This was the situation that the Road End boys found
themselves in during the spring of 1984. They didn't know that it would be the
end (well almost) of their European cup winning reign. Them foreign climbs
were rich picking for our lads, who knew how to work a till, as a few of them
had already worked in Butlin's and worked out how best to open the damn 'jack
and jill'. So, every one of the lads had to get on this decrepit train. Now, why the
authorities treated the football fans the way they did was obvious, you sow
what you seed. So, if a few of us smashed up the trains everybody would get
lumped into this pigeon hole of 'hooligans'. It certainly wasn't fair for them lot,
but they sort of got used to it in the end, and expected it. It was the classic 'self-
fulfilling prophesy', you tread youths like hooligans they are going to turn into

hooligans. It reminds me of education in the 70's. Some kids were instantly classified as having special needs and were immediately lumped together, they were bound to not achieve if they had no clever mates to ask, as the teachers didn't give a shit.

So they lumped us with all of the scarfers, and expected there to be no chaos. There is another principle, if you get one unruly kid in the class it sort of changes the mood, and everybody sees the lowest common denominator, and follows the loonies. So, the scarfers were expected to behave, despite the fact that everywhere we went, there was almost a guarantee that we would be attacked by away fans, especially after England fans kept causing chaos where ever they went. Liverpool fans always distanced themselves from England fans simply because everyone in England hated us and was a bit jealous of our success and we were the media darling. So, we have a great big stewing pot of nasty things happening together, and we were all in the middle, and they wanted us to behave, as if!

The station was buzzing even at this early hour, it was a long way to Rome and it was going to be a long, smelly journey. Now everybody was used to having a drink on the journey to the match, but everyone sensed a marathon session, and do you know what you are supposed to do at marathons, pace yourself.

Some lads simply didn't know how to pace themselves, as they looked at it this way. Ale = weekend = fun = pissed + the more the better.

So young people think that they can drink forever with no consequences, and that is what they did, but there were consequences.

Remo and Rod rolled up with brand new trainers, a pair of blue Adidas Grand Prix and a lovely pair of Adidas Munchen in White with red stripes. The tradition was always to wear your colours in Europe. The lads usually just wore a small metal badge, but red sun hats were the order of the day, Rod even had a chequered red and white flag to taunt rival fans. Remo had a cooler box full of tinnies of Stella, also a sandwich made by his mum. Rod had a little round tin for his ganga and that was about it, besides his deodorant and tooth brush. Young lads didn't really believe in hygiene at this age, just getting through the day and finding somewhere to slash.

"What time Gio and John getting down ?" Remo looked at his digital watch.

"Should be here now, they said something about cashing a giro before they got here". Rod was now working, so had to blag a few days off, by telling his boss that his granddad was on deaths door.

Gio and John turned up with brand new trainers on, John had a yellow and white tachini top on though, and it was a little bit bright. Gio had a sky blue Ellesse tracky top, they were both looking well smart, but they only had little bags with tooth brushes and sandwiches in.

"Fuckin' ell John you look like a cream slice with custard filling."

"Nice one Remo, your still an ugly cunt too".

Rod was ready to go "We ready to travel with the cavemen and aurld bastards, hope no one snores. Any birds on this train"?

"I hope not for their sakes, its gonna stink. I heard about the 77 trip, I hope they don't give us clapped out diesels with broken seats again".

"We're all off to sunny Rome, eviva e-Roma", Gio was excited.

"Where did ye get that song from Gio? I suppose it may stick after a few".

The train departed a full 36 hours before their arrival time in Rome, and it was a long, long journey. The lads were drinking all the way to Dover, then it was time to board the boat for Calais. The English leg was uneventful, the train was falling apart, when Rod went to sit down his wooden arm fell off and he started using it to throw at scarfers who were making too much noise.

The boat was always an adventure as there were shops on it, full of ale and bottles of spirits that fitted nicely into your inside pockets.

Gio and John went on the raid when the arcade slotties were empty. The constant noise of whirling, bleeping and twelve year old girls playing pacman was getting on John's nerves. They walked into the duty free away from the bar making sure no Scottish boys were around to offer them strange tablets again. The first stall offered single malt whiskey at half price. "See that John half price, I think that I should go for that, great bargain". Gio slotted one in his long pockets he had sewn into his nice Ellesse track suit top. John looked at him with a strange grin on his face. The boys raided a few more bottles of shorts and John was very tempted by the men's after shave. A lot of this stuff was in very small bottles for very expensive prices. John unlike Gio went for the most expensive stuff.

As the boys shuffled out, looking in all 360 directions like naughty schoolboys, John simply had to question Gio's logic. "Why did you get the ones on offer.

"Gio looked surprised that John didn't know "Out of principle of course. They reckon half price is good value, I reckon free price is better. So, I got one over on them. Maybe they'll think twice before pissing me off with shit offers next time".

John just simply shook his head, and they met up with the others by the bar. Remo was looking around for aggro already but he almost got used to the idea of taking the mickey out of the scarfers. Remo started throwing beer mats at the scarfers trying to knock one lads stupid tall hat off. The lad with the tall hat was that drunk that he didn't notice the attack, and started to flap at the beer mats like they were gnats attacking him. This highly amused Remo who was laughing his bollocks off. "What's he on la". John was eager for a fight, but there was nothing going on. In the end they found another Rugby team and decided to torment them. These lot were from Cambridge on a University outing.

"Alright lads, what's the score? Where you off to then", Rod was feeling chatty. "What's it to you Scouse"?

"Well, I thought if I talked to you first I wouldn't feel so guilty about twatting you gonks".

The captain stood up "Now look here, We may be big lads, but we know when we are outnumbered. There is no need for violence among men".

"How are you outnumbered there's only four of us, does each one of us count as two, ye daft posh twat".

Remo was still a bit pissed too and was laughing at the cheek of Rod.

"I don't mean that, I mean the whole boat is full of you Northern punks, I know when we are outnumbered. As soon as we retaliate, you lot will gel together like a bunch of bloody miners against the police".

"Northern punks I'm so offended mate". Remo was off on one now. He started to flick peanuts at the rugby team.

"These fuckin' scarfers are all pissed they've been drinking for hours now, and would rather have a good sleep than a barney with posh rugger dudes".

Gio just flipped then, I think he might have liked punks or just didn't like posh people. He flung a stool right at the biggest bastard in the team.

The stool bounced right off the top of his head, he just turned his head around like the terminator and looked straight at Gio. "Fuck he's a posh robot". Five of the rugby lads just couldn't help themselves they charged at Rod and he got rugby tackled to the floor. They started punching him. Remo grabbed another stool and smashed it over terminators head. It knocked him out cold then the other lot started to join in. Rod was having a go back and caught some posh nosh right in the face, his nose exploded. Rod jumped out of the way "Fuck off blood aids boy, you'se queers are always jumping on one another's arses". Remo got bored and chucked the peanut holder which hit some gonk in the chest. He stuck his chest out and simply said "Didn't hurt".

The fight was over before it started as the rugby boys were not biting, even though the scarfers hardly moved. A few ran over to see what the ruckus was. The boys went back over to duty free as it now had a small sports corner. There was nothing to rob though as it was all shit British gear, Hi-tech and Slazenger, shit for the posh twats who didn't have a clue. Remo grabbed a junior golf club and stuck it down his tracky bottoms, it made him walk like long john silver but he was kind of happy to have something to play with.

The European special was as bad as the English one. They must have found the shittiest carriages and said to one another "oui, le scousers will vandalise this, give them all the shit".

The call went up at the train station, it happened at every trip abroad, even the scarfers joined in "Calai, scalai, Calai, Scalai, Calai, Scally, We hate the frogs, we hate the frogs, ei di ey atio, We hate the frogs". Not that anybody knew any French people. It was an era when it was particularly trendy to be against anybody of different nationality, as globalisation and the EU was a distant dream.

As the stinky train crawled out of Northern France, they made a mistake of opening a bar on board, looking to cash in on these thirsty football lot. As everybody got settled and slowly more and more drunk it was time for nasty games. As lads fall asleep they will get attacked. On fat lad was asleep pretty quickly. Remo, John and Fergo held him down in case he struggled when awakened as Gio got a 3 pint jar of water and started to pour it over his head. He woke up instantly but the lads held him down. Basically he was water-boarded for about 45 seconds. When it was over he simply snorted the water over everyone in a mad panic he ran up and down the carriage snotting out water all over everyone. The lads couldn't help but laugh, and laugh for about three minutes. "What did you do that for you loonies"? Well you looked a bit de-hydrated mate, too much ale gives you dehydration". Another lad got all of his lovely locks cut off, Gio had bought a pair of scissors just for this task. This lad was proud of his long hair and thought that he was one of the scallies. Remo had the best way to wake him up, somebody had brought a bouncy ball that was frequently bounced all around the carriage, so Remo used his golf club to twat it straight at the lads head. He woke up in an instant. "What the fuck!" Then the chant started "1, 2, 3, 4, listen to the skinheads call, We want our hair back!"

"What you on about". He was looking around with his dizzy head trying to make sense of what was going on, then he felt his head. "Fuckers!, who did that". Again, they were rolling around on the floor laughing. As everybody got sleepy it was time for an involuntary farting contest. Some lads actually left the carriage and just kipped on the floor away from the smell. There was quite a few scousers with lovely thick moustaches the night before but had none the next day. As the train pulled into Rome, it was a long journey and there were some long and sore heads. The smell was unbearable as the trains only air conditioning was the small windows. Some lads had even wedged a door open for the last 50 miles to get some air and cool into the carriage. It looked like a bit of a shell when they got off. All of the light bulbs had been pulled out and smashed over random heads. Somebody had even brought a spray paint and re-painted one window red with the initials LFC Runcorn fingered in. I don't think the police even bothered checking it out, they already knew what it would look like. As Rod walked out he was that tired that the can stuck to his shoe, he just carried on walking making a clanking noise.

Rome was massive and boiling hot. Roma fans were everywhere. The atmosphere was decent at first, all the fans were in buoyant mood and the drinking carried on in the town square where Remo, Rod, Gio and John enjoyed the Italian sunshine which mixed well with the Italian beer. John had already sold his spirits so he had a bit of money for lager. But it was time for a bit of 'a stealing and a robbing' as the beastie boy's song goes.

There was some sterling sports shops, the lads started by stealing Head bags. The Italian shop staff must have been used to robberies as they were quite vidulant. But the sheer numbers of marauding scousers caught them out. There was about twenty in the lad's mob, they simply grabbed scousers from the square and suggested they knew where to get some good gear. It was as easy as that. A bit of Dutch courage and everybody was up for it. The mob simply stormed it grabbed what they wanted, filled their bags and stashed them somewhere quite secret. Some poor lad ended up using his local room as a storage area. Remo was getting excited and the tiring effect had not taken a hold of anybody yet, so it was time to go for a few tills. The first till was a sinch and the lads all shared out the booty. The second one was harder. As they stormed in, a man pulled the key out of the till. Fergo wrestled with the man trying his hardest to get the key off him, but credit to the Italian, he was not giving it up. He must have pressed some sort of alarm as the two-tone sound of the Italian pigs was close. Everyone simply bailed and left anything that they had grabbed. It was a close call and the end of stealing for the day.

The match was at 7:30 kick off and the mob was massive in the central square. The small Huyton contingent had grouped together with some other boys and they had went sight seeing before the match. The Trevi fountain was first stop and everybody simply jumped in singing football songs, as it was quite hot in the eternal city. The mood seemed to change as they got off the public transport for the stadium. As they stood there simply taking in the atmosphere, so sneaky Italian mopeds razzed past and some poor lad got his arse slashed. He was holding somebodies flag against it trying to stop the bleeding. The boys didn't expect this flash attack and it put everybody on alert for attacks.

The lads poured in to the stadium and the atmosphere was electric. For the first time Liverpool were not the dominant team in the stadium as somebody had the great idea of staging the final in Roma's home ground. The match was cagey and very close. But the fans made themselves heard, as we always did at every away ground. As Brucy did those wobbly legs, copied by Dudek years later, we finally won it. As this was most of the boys first Euro Final everybody went wild. Only John had been to the 78 final at Wembley against Bruges, but the Italians were not happy getting beat at home in such an important final. The first seeds of their Ultra's were very active that day and as soon as the scarfers got outside they were attacked from every angle. Now the police must have been half Roma fans as they didn't stop this attempted slaughter. About five scarfers were slashed on the arse. The onslaught was fierce and the boys just couldn't get to the front to defend our own fans. Eventually they got outside and it was pandemonium. Attacks were coming from every angle. The Road End boys pulled together about 50 boys and mounted a counter attack only to be attacked by the police. Every time we attacked the Italians moved away quickly and the police simply filled the void trying to grab any boys who were making a mark on the home hooligans. It was simply a loaded fight, on the Italians side. Eventually the boys broke away from the onslaught as it was pointless and everybody would have been arrested for defending ourselves. There were various newspaper reporters there that day, and they all seen exactly what happened, and thankfully reported it how they saw it. A joint attack from the police and the Italian fans. The crew of 50 managed to get away and chase Italians all over Rome, finally finding a pub to sit in and try to celebrate our great victory on foreign soils. But it was a cagey night, and half of the contingent had to leave at 11:30 to jump back on that smelly train.

The journey back was joyous at first, then we treated our bruises and most fell asleep for the whole journey to Calais, we were that knackered. There wasn't much messing on the way back even the teenagers were lacking any sort of energy. Nobody got back for the homecoming but there was bound to be more in the future, or so we thought. Some people say that this atmosphere lead to trouble in Heysel, and there could be some truth in this, but it still doesn't excuse holding a European cup final is such a dilapidated stadium, that and fifa where the major contributing factors that caused that terrible disaster. It killed hooliganism in England for a while and rightly so. Nobody should ever not come home from a match, it puts the whole business into perspective. As our own fans would also find out in 1989, when an equally terrible event happened. God bless all of those poor fans.

16

Arsenal at home

Very rarely will teams clash at stations in Merseyside but this one time it became a bit like London. Bristol City were playing Tranmere Rovers in Birkenhead and there would be a decent crew coming up. Now Bristol is a big city to have no top team, they did have one in the seventies, but not unlike Leeds they have now hit hard times. It was a day when nobody expected such a surprise crew turning up when the Road End boys were waiting for Arsenal to arrive.

It was busy in the station, and the lads were just loitering around. Most of the boys were in the Yankee bar on Lime Street. This was the main haunt for all reds as they waited for action to unfold outside. Not many crew's took that pub as it was a long and narrow place, not easy to storm at all. Remo and Fergo had a scam going whereby they would buy Marks and Spencers jumpers and t-shirts and sew genuine La Coste crocodiles on them. The genuine jumpers cost over £90 so they were making a fair profit off their fellow scalls. They would even change the label on the back.

Arsenal usually had a big crew these days, being one of the big teams in London would always guarantee numbers.

Doyley and Boiler were propping up the bar, and the drinks were flowing at about 12 noon. Rod, John and Gio were wetting their whistles drumming up a big of Dutch courage, but there were massive numbers today. There was about 200 boys outside and 50 in the pub. A load ended up the vines and the Crown Hotel. Now Liverpool being a massive club also had massive numbers on certain days. The visit of the big teams always gave a big turnout. London trains were due every hour and the police knew by this year that a load would get the ordinary train.

This LFC crew knew that they could easily break through police lines, the risk of a few arrests was worth the ruckus. It seemed that a lot of people hated Arsenal too, as big teams were usually hated the most. The gunners were in the top 5 and this usually increased the rivalry. The only other team coming close to the reds in the league this year were Southampton, and although they could pull numbers on special occasions their crew was small in comparison.

"I fuckin' hate arsenal, you'd think I was born a Jew, the way I hate them." Remo was in a narky old mood.

"Why, do ye hate them Remo lad!" Rod was swigging down Newcastle Brown, he always drunk this in this pub as the bottles would come in handy, very big bottles in an emergency.

"Fuckin' toe-rags, who pick on smaller numbers I reckon. Last time I encountered them they tried to cut up all my best gear, with me in it, I dunno, it almost makes me want to use a knife, if they do. What am I supposed to do"? A big roar went off outside and you could see somebodies head getting bashed against the Yankie bar window.

The lads all ran outside and all you could see was battles in the street, it seemed like 200 on to 200. Even numbers and the police were too scared to rush in, they were too few and knew when to let it die down a bit. But this wasn't dieing down. Remo steamed in and immediately got flattened by some big bovver boot. Rod ran over to help but got a sign smashed against his head. Now this was descending into a Lime Street riot. It was obvious who was who as this crew had skin-head clothes on and they were was a lot of older lads. Some even had team colours on and scarfs. "The cheek of these cunt's, what the fuck are they scarfers or boys? I thought skin heads had died out in the seventies". The cars all stopped the riot was that bad some feller got out of his car and ran away. It was one of those round cars, a VW beetle. The Road End boys decided to get in and drive at the cave dwellers. But when they got near the opponents they sort of chickened out running them over. Now this was a mistake as the cave dwellers decided to turn the car over with the scallies inside. Remo started to take photos as he was starting a violence scrapbook. There was still fighting going on all around him and he just wanted a record of the ruck. John steamed into the away fans and grabbed the hot dog stand bowl of steaming water. He lashed it straight at the Bristol. That's who they were, they wanted to surprise everyone, including the police. They had managed to scramble over a fence away from the waiting police who expected Arsenal. It was a fabulous fight. Some Bristol were now being battered inside the ABC Cinema. A group of about 30 scalls had cornered them inside the cinema foyer. They all ended up running in the picture rooms and were chased around the seats. Some cinemagoers even recall shadows running past the screen, some lad felt like clapping, which people actually did do in the cinema after a film years ago. It was like a scene from the game Duke Nuke 'em . The boys knew that Bristol had had enough inside the pictures so they helped themselves to big tubs of popcorn and walked out like they had just seen a violent film. Outside was more like serious Sam with everybody still smashing into one another. There was quite a lot of blood on people's faces and a group ran into St Johns shopping precinct after the Bristol

City bovver boys. Some Bristol climbed on top of a bus stop trying to get away from the scousers, and some ran into the kitchen of the local chippy. They grabbed polythene cones and filled them with hot fat and started chucking them at their attackers, who quickly retreated. Some nutter even found a clever and ran after a load of lads with it. The police quickly grabbed him, their own bravery admired by the fans. However, Bristol surged back and loads of reds ran back into their pubs and some even into the Adelphi foyer. The fighting carried on and there was some road works at the bottom of Mount Pleasant (I know a strange name for a street). A few Bristol got in the hole in the road which was surrounded by orange and white barriers and started lobbing lumps of mud at anybody and everybody. Remo ran over to look down the hole, and they looked like First World war soldiers in the trench, their faces were covered in mud. Remo couldn't help but start laughing at them as they chucked lumps of mud in his direction. Rod ran over with his supplies for the day and chucked in a red smoke bomb. The soon all started piling out there was about five of them, coughing their guts up. Still the police had not got control, they seemed to have control of the station and the Crown Hotel and Yankee bar. So, the hooligans couldn't get out to join in. Still the street was crowded with fans, and all the cars still couldn't move. A few windows went in, it was the Bristol fans just getting frustrated, they even had the audacity to smash the jewellers, and they even ran into a menswear shop and came out with bowler hats on. If they were fans of clockwork orange this was a sure sign. These fans were well up for it. The scousers managed to surge back into them, as they piled out of the Vines and the Adelphi foyer. Some lad had stolen the bus boys cloak and staff and was chasing Bristol lashing out with this metal decorative staff. Still the fight carried on it must have been ten minutes of pure fighting. But the Liverpool boys were renowned for being hard and didn't give in easily. The managed to chase the Bristol City up the big hill towards the University. But by the time they were at the top of the hill both the scousers and the Bristol City were knackered from the hill climb and the fight, and the police restored control. The Liverpool boys were marched back to their pubs where they would be occupied with drinking, and talking about the barney. Bristol City were all marched down to Liverpool Central station where they were hurried onto the underground, and given over to the Wirral force and off the hands of Liverpool police. They simply didn't have enough men to cope with this new threat. They did make a mistake sending the The Road End boys back to Lime street pubs though, they simply should have cleared them out of the area as the London ordinary was about to arrive.

Rod and Remo now walking into the Vines. This pub has massive ornamental decorations in every direction and a great big ornamental ceiling. If you ever come straight into Lime street it is well worth a visit, just to see a work of art. Arsenal stormed off the train, which was also half wrecked, now there was about 150 of them and they were pure boys. So, the half fight was on again, and this time the cockneys were up for it. There were a few spotters who stormed straight into the Vines, Yankee bar and the Crown to warn everybody about the invasion. Everybody surged out at once, the police were a bigger force now and managed to separate the warring factions. Police horses stormed in and separated fans by almost smashing into their feet. There was another force of reds expecting the police to do this behind the lines. About 40 lads steamed into the Arsenal, a few lads had lumps of wood and wooden sticks, they smashed straight into the back of the gunners, who responded in kind. The bizzies grabbed a few scousers and the rest retreated into the shopping centre. There was another crew in the under road link subway, they stormed out right in the middle Arsenal and chaos ensued for about 30 seconds until the police dogs and handlers charged the attack back down the subway. Liverpool would not give up this day and managed to follow the convoy of supporter's right up Scotland Road, taunting them and lobbing pieces of debris when the bizzies were not looking. There were a few raids from local scallies as well, and three cockneys who decided to exit the convoy got battered and taxed of their trainers.

Five lads where having a bomb fire inside one of the tenement blocks and decided to run down with burning sticks and lobbed them straight into the middle of the cockneys. Sparks flew everywhere as the cockneys looked like they were being bombed by the Taliban. A group of police chased the loonies away and called the fire brigade. Liverpool were really in the mood on this day and the convoy suddenly bumped into another group of Road End boys who started to launch bricks and coins in their midst. The coppers didn't know what to do as the missiles were launched from multiple directions. As they reached the Anfield Road the attack stopped and it was time for business to resume inside Anfield. If anybody has ever been in the Anfield Road End it was more or less all seats by this time. Originally, there was standing room but it was quickly seated to reduce the trouble and give the illusion of comfort to the visiting cowboys. The left corner was allocated to the away fans. From the first minute, it was a coin throwing competition. The Arsenal even got some from the Kemlin Road stand, where a few lads used to sit now and again. The Arsenal fans started to look a bit edgy and returned every insult with renewed vigour. A few seats started getting lobbed from the away end straight into the Road End. The boys took exception to this and steamed towards the dividing fence. This was a manic day as the fence started to get pulled down by the Road End boys. Eventually it came down as stewards where knocked out of the way for spoiling the fun. The police couldn't seem to get near the trouble and that's when the two sets of boys clashed. With it only being a small entry the fight seemed to stall at the small opening. Different lads took turns to steam in and smash someone in the face. Arsenal seemed to have the same tactics and there were a lot of big black lads ready for a go. Eventually the bizzies retained control but the threat of violence seemed to hang about all during the first half.

Rod, John, Remo, Gio, Yoggie, Julien and Fergo were sticking together, and almost everybody needed the bog. They all stormed down at once, and some other boys decided to latch on, as it looked like another possible raid. Now in the 80's the toilets were the only place where opposition fans could meet without a fence between them. Arsenal were already waiting and a big kick off started again. Lanny and Kinny were about and liked to flash the steel. Two Arsenal were instantly down holding their arms, their arms were caked in blood. The boys all realised that they didn't want to blamed for this nasty attack and they steamed back out of the bogs, after exchanging a few blows with the cockneys.

As the second half started the roar went up from Arsenal. "You dirty stabbing bastards, you dirty stabbing bastards".

As soon as the match was about to finish there was a stampede of coloured trainers towards the exit. And the boys all left early. There were some hand communications with Arsenal who seemed to get the idea to go outside now. The cockneys were really riled up because of what had happened and immediately caught the scousers off guard. The scousers simply had to run, the attack was so ferocious. The Arsenal chased us onto Stanley park. This was going to be a big pitch battle. The bizzies got wind of what was going on and the charge of the light brigade horses joined in the ruckus.

Some big fat lad about six foot five stated to boot Rod, and his two mates looked for an easy prey. Remo, John and Gio were fighting just behind this and they all turned around when they heard the painful cries of crunching kicks to the abdomen. Remo tried to do his special thump on top of the head, but this fat gooner was simply too tall. Remo did a karate kick instead but it seemed to just ripple his fat belly. Gio and John attacked the two other lads, who looked like tough opponents. John wasn't winning but Gio smashed into his foe with some fist force. Gio smashed the tall feller in the back of the head and Rod got up and kicked him in the balls at full pelt. Rod's Burberry jacket was all ripped, he was more concerned about this that the fact his nose was all over the map. "You cockney cunt you owe me, me mar's gonna kill me mate". Gio yanked the tall fella's coat of him as he tried to leg it the other way. This made him stumble over. Gio handed the coat straight to Rod, but he looked at it disgustingly. "What the fuck it that Adidas shit, I grew out of that two years ago, besides it's three sizes too big". Gio looked at him funny "Suit ye fuckin self you fussy git, I'll have it then". Gio put it on, even though he was six foot the arms came over his fingers, and the jacket was green. John turned around after smacking somebody else. "Fuckin ell Gio, you look like the jolly green giant".

The police regained control and the mobs were dispersed in different directions. The lads all walked over to the cabbage and finished off the day with a few songs, and shared memories of who twatted the most cockneys. This was one action packed day, and wouldn't be repeated for a while. But it was fun while it lasted.

17

Chelsea and Millwall away

One of our epiphanies within Violence came on a Saturday morning in 1985. Chelsea were flying after a decent season and were in the top 4, together with West Ham, Everton and Sheffield Wednesday. The reds simply had get that title, as we were at our peak. Also, the violence had intensified and now it was every club with a casual firm. Times were exciting, dangerous and about to get out of hand.

The biggest crew for months was upstairs on the roof area for Lime Street station.

The funniest part was Trout a lad from Kirkdale had brought his dog along. Now it wasn't a big dog, it was a Jack Russell, and it could bite. It was given to him by his cousin only three weeks prior to this trip so he wasn't too bothered if he lost it or not. He saw it as a weapon against other fans.

Remo had got geared out in the best stuff he ever bought. He had Armani jeans, a lovely stripy lacoste t-shirt, Lyle and Scott jumper in dark purple and a Beige Burberry jacket and scarf, topped off with a Ellesse bucket hat in red. Rod was similar to Remo but had Rockport boots and a fishing jacket. Gio was still into Ellesse track suits and La coste bubble coat. John still had his Tacchinni sky blue track suit top, Lee jeans and Adidas Gazelle in green.

Trout was more into music and had a Genesis T-shirt on, guess Jeans and a pair of old Kios boots from the start of the 80's.

The dog did a shit and Remo was complaining to Trout that is stunk. Trout didn't have any bags or spades so he picked it up with his fingers and threw it down towards the road. Everybody was calling him for all the scruffy bastards as he washed his hands in a pool of nearby rainwater. He had watched the shit splatter in front of some office dudes, who looked very puzzled, like a giant pigeon was loose somewhere.

Rod had gotten hold of some new ganga off a bike black rasta down in Granby called 'bunny'. Rod had now progressed to a Sherlock Holmes pipe and sometimes wore a trilby to complement the look when he walked around his home town. He was stuffing it with all sorts on this day, lovely moist black Moroccan draw, it was wrapped in foil to keep the freshness in.

The lads were now sitting in the circle passing it around. The dog was in the middle of them looking sheepish so nobody else shouted at it for crapping everywhere. Remo and Rod had Sony walkman's with The Jam and Supertramp playing. Gio looked up and noted that a piece of metal girder was falling form the roof. John decided that he wanted this old station to fall down and managed to climb into the station itself and push the girder slightly so it fell 50 foot to the floor. He shouted 'Timbar' in case any poor sods were underneath it. As it fell everybody watched it go, it felt like slow motion and some of the lads were holding their heads in dread if it hit somebody. It crashed with a massive clang to the floor and left a one foot dint in the concrete. Everybody started laughing as the station people all looked up and conversed as to how this could have happened. John was still hiding behind the concrete trying not to fall off as the push had unbalanced him a bit. He crawled back over to the lads who gave him a clap except Trout who mentioned that it fucking stupid and he could have killed someone.

Remo was on a high again and was daring Trout to jump 25 foot to the next floor, Remo said that he would give him his new Fred Perry jumper if he did it. Trout was really temped as he was proper skint. He saw himself as a bit of a stuntman, and looked the part with his long blond locks and gangly body.

The lads all made a build up noise as he got ready, his arms in the air like a long jumper getting ready for something special. He charged towards the window and actually made the leap. It was insane he landed and did some sort of Para roll. The lads all cheered as his sprung back up, then fell down holding his foot. He limped back up the metal staircase "Fuck that was a big drop, Fred Perry you say Remo". Over time the station built up and this was going to be a mammoth mob. There must have been 400 boys in the station. The lad's upstairs were still in a circle waiting their mates to arrive downstairs. The pot was strong today and five of the lads used the echo of the old station to sing a version of "In the blue ridge mountains of Virginia", with one lad doing a Stan Laurel and varying the pitch of the song, to the amusement of everyone in the station who must have thought it was a new fangled PA system. Some div tried to give the dog a puff but he was having none of it. Gio had brought a leather ornate catapult and some bull bearings to fit in it. He sneaked down the stairs and waited while John and Rod followed him down to watch. As two bizzies walked past he pulled the trigger. The bull bearing must have been half an inch and twatted him right on the bobbies helmet with a popping noise. His helmet topped over and the nipple broke off the top. The lads all burst out into silent laughter and they walked back up the stairs. The next target was a copper sitting down having a break. He seemed to have a pasty. Gio pulled the trigger again, this time it hit him full in the balls. He made a loud groan and fell to the ground holding his crutch. The whole gang burst out into laugher except Trout who was worried about repercussions. The police were running all over the station for somebody with a pellet gun, but they would never find anybody on the ground floor.

After another half an hour the lads all tumbled down the stairs and were greeted by the biggest mob you have ever seen. The police were by this year informed of what was going on, but due to personal freedoms could not stop anybody from traveling on trains. The mob had to pile onto two different trains as the first one was completely full. Now trains used to run every half hour between the two big cities, and this was going to be a trip to remember. Extra guards were ordered and the boys more or less had the whole of the first train with others normal passengers being rescheduled after warnings of the risks of traveling with lunatics by the police.

The destination was Stamford Bridge again, and the train was bouncing with singing, as everybody let loose with Ale flying everywhere and a lot of ammunition was stored under the seats ready for the cockneys.

The main song was stolen from Chelsea's one man went to mo, but the words were changed to "Chelsea we will go, killing cockney bastards. Scousers are abroad, hunting for head hunters".

The lads where doing some sort of terrace jump all together in the middle carriage, the carriage was shaking each time they jumped together it felt like it was leaving the rails at 90mph, a bit scary. Then the call went up 5,4,3,2,1, LEFT! Everybody jumped to the left of the carriage and the carriage almost come off its rail again. Some more nervous lads charged into another carriage thinking it was actually going to happen.

The driver was actually told not to stop at the usual stations by the on-board police, who were dictating what exactly happened to these boys. Now the lads knew what was happening and were not happy, it meant no fights with other fans at the stations along the way. Kingy was another nutter who liked to cause havoc, so he waited until they were coming up to a town called Lemmington Spa, but he mis-judged the stop and they ended up near a village just before the stop. He yanked on the emergency brake and the whole train cheered. It was quite a hot day so the lads all piled out to do a piss as one of the bogs was blocked up and look for something else to do.

The victims of the mischief were two cows. About twelve lads chased the cows who were actually quite big when you got up close to them. Kingy managed to evade one cow pat, but the next one he slipped on almost knocking his face out of joint. He got up embarrassed as if nothing had happened, then carried on chasing the black and white beast. The lads then surrounded one cow and Kingy jumped on. He somehow managed to keep the cow calm while another lad controlled the other cow. The police were actually just watching them laughing, so much for the law. Then the two cows were lined up and some lad smacked them both on the arses and they bolted. Kingey was hanging on for dear life and the other lad instantly did a summersault off the back if the best and landed on his arse, he rubbed his arse and got up, and ran after the cow.

Kingey lasted about 30 seconds with his arm in the air, and the whole train cheered and the driver waited for the loonies to finish their fun. The police then came into action as soon as a red tractor started to appear from the horizon. The lads were all waved back onto the train, and the driver found the need to carry on. A few lads tried the emergency brakes again, but fuck health and safety the driver must have turned it off.

As the train approached Euston, the lads got ready to charge past the pigs. Just before it jilted to a stop all doors were flung open and the charge began to hop the gates to freedom. The police must have had 20 on duty but they simply couldn't handle this amount of lunatics. A massive roar went up and there was 20 West Ham already in the station. 300 boys all stormed over the gates, normal passengers scattered everywhere at the riot. West Ham scattered into every other direction just like the normal people. It looked like a marathon running straight through the station as everybody had trainers on and lots of coloured sports gear and ski coats. They stormed outside and charged down into a subway kicking every hoarding on the way, and pulling mad faces at the passers-by. It was pandemonium, and some poor busker got his guitar robbed and then slung at a dirty old tramp. The plan originally meant waiting for the second train but this just wasn't happening, a quick plan was hatched to contact each other through London phone boxes, numbers were exchanged and this would be Liverpool's first organised firm violence. The plan was to storm Millwall's place then move on to Chelsea, so the massive firm had to calm down when they reached the subway and get the first train to South London, Surrey Quays. So the plan was the change at Whitechapel. As the lads passed Liverpool Street they couldn't help but burst into a chorus of "Liverpool, Liverpool, Liverpool street".

At Whitechapel it was a mass change, and they had to wait for two other trains to let off, before they were all together again, which didn't make much sense as they would need to divide again to fill more trains. The underground was filled with the chorus of "Scousers here, scousers there, scousers every fucking where". There was talk of Spurs and Arsenal being about but nobody saw anybody, it may have just been a few scarfers or bits and pieces of casuals meeting up before their trip. Then they started piling on to the Millwall train, there was a few Milwall scarfer's who quickly took off their scarfs and sat on them, but the scousers were not after them so they were left well alone. Still no police had caught up with the scouse hoards, and this was going to be a riot as soon as they all met up again. The only problem they had was not being able to re-group in time, so Millwall would be informed and the bushwackers would be on the way to face a smaller crew. The weaponry was extensive this day, these boys knew that they needed it to face the awesome reputation of Millwall. The lads found a pub on the corner of Hawkstone Road, which is now called The Yellow House, with a field behind. They divided themselves up, half sat on the field and the other half went inside the pub. Some lads started looking for mushrooms to fill the time, the others sat under a tree, there was about 100 on the field. Some little kids came over on BMX bikes and started asking who are you on this field? and what they wanted. They were told to 'fuck off', and did as they were told. There were also some break dancers doing their stuff that seemed to entertain the lads, who enjoyed the show and encouraged the young black and white cockneys to show some more. The second train full arrived and it was the whole crew together again. They walked down Rotherine New Road towards the stadium hoping to find a boozer to smash up. This crew was massive and just before the railway bridge they found about 20 young casuals waiting around by some scruffy council houses. The whole mob chased them through the tunnel, which stopped all of the traffic each way. They swarmed after the 20 past some scruffy council flats on the right, where prying eyes were watching them. Straight past some scruffy industrial estate, and they say Liverpool is a dump. Under another railway bridge then they swarmed left down some other crappy street called Ilderton Road towards the Lions Den. More dodgy looking council estates and it started to feel like they were in their element. Just by another little arch they found a pub and it was filled with Milwall. They stormed outside and smashed every window. They had so many weapons and the police were about now. There were about 30 bushwhackers in the pub and they were big fellers, and also armed with everything they could find. They looked battle hardened, and scared from head to toe. Some of them even looked like body builders, all trunk and arms, and no hair.

It seemed this place was teaming with London casuals up for the battle. These lads had a real go though. But they were outnumbered ten to one, and this was one day Millwall would have to face defeat. There was a surge of scousers, storming inside and attacking the bushwhackers with all of their weapons. They had coshes and knuckdusters, Stanley knives and bricks. Everything went at the cockneys, and they simply couldn't do anything because of the size of this scouse invading army. The crew knew that they had done Milwall and charged back to the station before the coppers could restrain them, which would have been an effort anyway.

Blue lights and sirens were everywhere around the smashed up pub and poor bushwhackers who were not expecting any scousers this day or any other day, as they were totally in a different league.

Now it was Chelsea's turn to feel the scouse army's wrath. Chelsea had put on a really good show at Anfield that year and revenge was on the cards. The lads knew not go back to the original station as this would have got back to the police, so it was off to the other side of South London for two results in one day. Straight to South Bermondsey. They all piled on to a massive train and it was off to Central London and Bond Street. Everyone was ecstatic that they had done Milwall even though they only did a small crew who wasn't ready, it was the bushwhackers and they did get done. One for the scrapbook that one, I wonder if that's why it's called a scrapbook. The whole crew decided to surface at Bond Street to see what there was to steal in this built up shoppers paradise. The sports shops were now avoided as they were too well guarded and CCTV'ed up. It was the jewellers that were the target now. The crew somehow came out on Oxford Street shopping centre, the first Jewellers they found about 100 lads stormed in and simply swiped everything from under the cases, some cases where smashed and the security was overwhelmed, this was just like a cartoon Tasmanian devil attack. Everyone stuck jewellery in every orifice and pocket they could stuff them into. A second jewellers over the road was done, after trying unsuccessfully to smash the window, they simply did a smash and run attack inside. The whole mob caused chaos on the main shopping street and shoppers were running everywhere to get out of the way, except three old tramps who followed them in and got a bit themselves. This time it was back to Bond Street station as it was on the correct line for Fulham Broadway station. As the crew were about to get on the train the chant went up but it was louder than ever "The Road End, The Road End!". Now one lad was ahead of the curve when it came to technology, and had a great big heavy piece of electronics. A few lads asked if it was some sort of metal brick weapon, but no it wasn't, it was a 1980's mobile telephone. He was actually on the blower to his mate who had a similar device on the second Euston train. They had arrived and the idea was to co-ordinate their attack on the Chelsea head-hunters who were now a well-established crew on par with the ICF.

The lads were all fascinated with this mobile phone, which actually had a retractable aerial. Songs were sung on the train, this mob felt unbeatable and it was soon to get bigger. Wood Lane Station and still no police stops, this was going to be a massacre. The second crew were waiting around another hundred lads ready to raid.

Remo was rubbing his hands "Come on lads, lets do Chelsea....again". Rod cheered and dropped his pipe which was still lit after all this time. Rod had three rings on him and Remo a thick gold necklace. Gio and John had got a ring each, Gio's was full of red ruby's he was thinking about putting it on to keep it from being lost, but It might also get broke. Rod passed around the pipe and it seemed to go around about 30 lads, lot of them unknown to him but happy to be part of the party. John was on a high just for the buzz of smashing cockneys, this invading army was on par with the Vikings or the Mongolian hoards. It was time to take the capital again. Some lad had even put horns on a bicycle helmet expecting such a big turnout.

And so, the initial charge happened the shops were ignored it was time to do Chelsea. There were about five pubs on the Fulham Road, the first pub got turned over in what seemed like three minutes. The till got smashed, every cockney seemed to run out, they simply were not prepared for 400 scouse boys on the prowl. The second put contained no boys again, so was trashed and robbed within seconds, that's when the sirens started to wine up. It also alerted Chelsea and their head hunters to some action. There was one pub with about 45 Chelsea boys in who stormed out to see what the fuss was all about. They must have been shocked to see 400 scousers running at them with sticks and weapons, ready to splatter anybody and everybody in their way. To their credit they stood for about thirty seconds and fought until they realised this was a country level invasion. They ran for their lives when the Stanley boys pointed their knives in the air. The chase began, and Chelsea were re-enforced from every corner but it was never going to be enough, it was just more Chelsea running. The next pub was trashed and jack and jill opened and the cops were now getting a gauge of how many Liverpool were invading. The noise from the invading army was scary, but the vans started to arrive, and Chelsea did the unthinkable, it was a brave and game move by them to turn and face us, but turn they did. They must have realised that the cops were about to get a handle on the situation. That's when the fight for Fulham Road happened. The clash was brutal on both sides. Remo stormed in as usual, and started kicking out, in his usual manner. Rod knew it was now time to fold up his Sherlock and get stuck in, only problem was he forgot to put it out. He stormed at some stripey cockney headhunter who was far too big for him to handle, but he looked awesome with smoke bellowing from his shirt, the Chelsea man didn't know what to make of him. He was getting beat until another red intervened, then another, then another. This was going to be a one way battle. John smashed somebody over the head with what looked like a brick and he was instantly a floppy doll fall to the ground. Gio was having a ball and taking on three Chelsea on his own as he knew that he had instant backup. The Chelsea were now getting battered, but the scousers were happy that they had something to fight. The police presence were getting ready to charge in, and Chelsea started to retreat. One hundred Chelsea started jumping over road barriers and the bizzies moved in with dogs. The battle was over. There were about ten cockneys all over the road lying down, with one unconscious. The dogs came in and bit a few scousers, as this is what the police wanted. One dog got booted in the teeth and quickly retreated from the mob. There were weapons thrown all over the road. Behind the hoard was a barrage of broken windows. The mob riot was a full blown scary sight. There was even a car turned over, the lads had got really excited and wanted to emulate Toxteth in 81 at one stage. The battle was over and Police were called in from many neighbouring districts. The Road End army was marched into Stamford Bridge, but there was to be no more fun this day, as the damage was done. The mood inside the ground was joyous, the Road End army sang for hours without break, they were in the greatest of moods having trashed two of London's biggest firms in one day. This kind of destructive day would never be repeated as security got tighter, police more and more organised and CCTV was an instrumental weapon in stopping anonymous chaos from reigning.

18

11 October 1986 Cardiff vs Wrexham + Scousers

Earlier in this book we mentioned about Chester befriending The Road End boys. But the scousers were nothing but non-conformist, this is the story of a particular friendship with Wrexham, and how they challenged their southern neighbours, who constantly called them 'more Scouse than Welsh'. Although their accent obviously does contain some scousisms and a touch of the accent it was a statement that really got up Wrexham's nose, they felt as Welsh as Cardiff, Swansea and Newport who were all the Welsh representation in the English league. Really, it should be called the English and Welsh league, but let's save that argument for another day.

The boys promised to meet up with Wrexham in Chester as that was the general route South to Cardiff. It was a really cold October day and the wind wasn't letting up. Thank god that the in thing these days was to wear thick ski coats. There was probably a sensible reason for this, as those terraces were not exactly wind resistant.

The boys took the Liverpool underground for a change, which is one of only three in the country. When they arrived in Chester there was already a fight going on in the station. There was a standoff between Wrexham and Chester fans. Now if you know anything about derbies then this is one of the least known but most fierce. The rivalry is based on border fighting that spans back a thousand years, when the English used to pillage the Welsh Villages, and the Welsh would return the favour. Chester and York were the Capitals of Northern England for a long time, so big armies used to invade the Welsh hills. Wrexham being the Capital town of North Wales was probably their biggest rivals. So, as father tells son about those damn English, the legends live on and so does the hatred.

The English were actually getting the better of Wrexham and nobody would usually expect your fellow English to attack one another to defend a different nation, but this is exactly what happened during the next ten minutes. The forty Liverpool lads stormed at Chester who were caught off guard and simply had to make a tactical retreat. It was one like of those mornings when you have just woke up and someone punches you straight in your face. Half the crew were still half asleep and it was quiet on the train down there. You have to instantly gee yourself up, and adrenaline is the best drug for this particular task.

Remo ran straight into Chester and varied his attack today by performing a massive shoulder barge. Remo was very decent at football and was trying out some on the field moves. Rod copied him but did a sliding tackle across the polished station floor with his dusty bottomed Adidas Munich trainers. He knocked some Chester lad clean off his feet and followed up with a swift smack to his jaw before retreating and waving his arms like he had scored a goal.

Fergo had a fisherman's rope with a net full of bullbearings and was swinging it around trying to catch somebody. He caught a Chester lad right on his ankles, he screamed with pain, but five Chester saw what happened and instantly attacked Fergo with their fists. He was not ready as the swing took a bit of time to start up. He went down like a German fighter pilot, but Wrexham saw what happened and chased away the attackers. The station was then empty of Chester, who must have felt rather pissed off to be double attacked without notice. A lad called Jumble was one of the Wrexham leaders and got Fergo to his feet. "Good timing scouse, we were a bit under the cosh there".

"Yeh, how come they were here". Fergo replied

"About that, we arranged a row with them, but under estimated their numbers. We were on their turf, so we should have expected it, but we did think you might be here earlier".

"It's alright, we haven't had it off with Chester yet. The Tranmere lads let us know how much fun it is against them though. They reckon it's one of those towns with loads of gays in, but they do seem half decent. Think it might be their Blacon boys who rule the roost down there."

"Yeh, we hate Chester, but what about Cardiff, I think we might just hate them southerners even more, they really think that they are the only place in Wales. We even teamed up with the Swan Jacks one week to tear into them. I think it's a capital city thing, a bit like what the cockneys are for you'se lot".

The combined crews numbered one hundred boys. The Wrexham lot were 80% casuals, but some skinheads and about ten lads who worked on farms and had big arms, massive stature and big attitudes to violence.

The train was full of commuters, but did stop at a few relevant cities on the way. Birmingham was usually a flashpoint as the stop usually lasted ten minutes to let valuable passengers board. About half of the lads got off to buy some snacks and steal some more. At the shop counter was twenty casuals, who were actually West Brom. Both sides froze, then Rod and Remo threw some full cans straight at them which missed them all, and exploded against a magazine rack. The Albion didn't realise how many mixed casuals were in attendance and attacked the scouse, Welsh mix. They made a great play of it, and the Liverpool/Wrexham boys pulled back a little, until they were re-enforced with more lads who saw people running. West Brom then looked desperate as they were cornered. One of their nutters fronted up the mob and had hold of a barbecue fork. A few lads backed off then he threw it. It hit some lad called Boiler right in the calf, and stuck dead in his leg. He let out a bit of a scream, and West Brom made a dash for the doors. A few lads were tripped up and kicked all over the floor. They escaped and the lads knew they needed to board the train again or miss the Welsh confrontation. Poor boiler went straight to Birmingham infirmary and was sorted out but was sick to miss the action. The next few stops were all small towns so the crew didn't bother getting off. The atmosphere was good and friendly as Liverpool didn't often mix with other crews, but these lads were more or less local to North West England and considered Liverpool as their main city for shopping and partying, they almost admitted to being a bit scouse. As the train pulled into Cardiff Ninian Park Station it was time for fun.

The Soul Crew are a well-established crew and anyone who wants to challenge them will need a decent crew and will power to see it through. There was a crew of thirty already waiting for any Wrexham as they had simply twatted Wrexham because of their small numbers over the years. Today was going to be different. The soul crew stood for a couple of minutes and gave it their best, but the English/Welsh crew stormed into them and knocked two unconscious before the police stormed in and took some form of control. But the crew were not going to be restrained quite so easily and quickly scarpered from the police and sloped up Sloper Road, and into Jubilee Recreation Ground. On the field there must have been one hundred Soul Boys Crew, and this battle would now become an even playing field.

Remo stormed the whole crew towards them "Come on, lets have these Welsh bastards". "Hang on lad, were Welsh too, but I get your point, lets go", a Wrexham head shouted. The soul crew didn't expect such a big band of lads and were probably confused as to why Wrexham had such a crew. The clash was ferocious, and a about five lads went down in the initial clash. Two lads on each side were instantly slashed across their bodies. The combined force seemed to be gaining the advantage though. And the soul crew were suddenly on the defensive, throwing bricks and stones while they ran towards the main road. The Wrexham lads were joyous at the result, but all wasn't over.

The scousers were battle hardened and didn't usually ever give in on a good fight. The police again arrived, two police vans stormed onto the field and three horses, charged the combined force. The crew followed the soul boys and everybody clashed again on the road. Cardiff, Liverpool, Wrexham it was a big melee. Some scouser had raided a local kitchen and about ten plates were Frisbeed at the Welsh catching one poor lad on his head, which burst open with spurting blood. Unfortunately, for the combined crew that's as good as it got. Their little victory was short lived. The soul crew were boosted in numbers four fold and it had become dangerous.

Constant waves of attacks even right through a police line started. These were battle hardened nutters. Three police went down as they stormed into the crew, Remo went down with a cut to his arm, probably someone lashing out with a blade. Rod had a cut on his ear, he mentioned it was somebody with a big sovereign ring. Gio was limping as somebody had thrown a brick at his knee, and he was struggling. They were taking a battering. John was the only one untouched by injury, probably only because he was like a possessed rat, at five foot six he was nimble enough to scramble out of a situation and get a few digs in too. The Wrexham lot were fighting with passion, at every wave of Cardiff they would defend their ground with every ounce of energy they had. There was a few bloodied and bruised Wrexham. As Wrexham and Liverpool were ushered into the ground, they were still being attacked from the rear; the police simply couldn't handle the numbers. Inside the stadium there was a lot of posturing by both sets of fans.

Rod had his ear covered in plasters which the St Johns ambulance lot gave him. Gio had a big bandage around his leg and his jeans were all rolled up. "Them fucking nutters, they were really up for it though, I'll give it to them. This place is a shed though Remo."

Remo had a bandage on his arm "Yeh, these lot are a bit mad. We need to come back next year with a bigger crew, they've fuckin' ruined my new Ellesse ski coat, if I knew it would be this bad then I would have arranged more numbers, how are you Rod".

Rod had just skinned up, he didn't care if he was in the middle of a public place. Besides he was in Wales and that usually meant he was on holiday and it was time to relax. "I'm sound mate, I agree though Remo, We need more numbers here, nobody told us that Cardiff were hard, who would have expected that".

19

Extra bits and Ethics

I have done quite a bit of dj'ing in my time and as we all try to earn a crust we come across violent people and even family gangs. Some families actually think that they are a crew in their own right. Then there are weddings, which can end just as violently as any match. It's the combination of putting together long lost people who have long standing vendettas and grudges against each other, mix this with alcohol. One time I was trying to get payed and there was a mighty battle going on outside a club in Fazakerly. I asked the mother of the bride who calmly replied that "As soon as the fight has finished I'll get you your money off him". It's just a good job that he won.

Another time I booked a family who were big into supplying drugs and guns, who flat refused to pay me, I simply put it down as a learning experience and changed my payment method and in what districts I would do work.

I once encountered some Man United fans who decided to spit at me at the end of the night for playing YNWA. This problem with this record happened a lot especially with Everton fans, but I did like to rile them up and show my loyalties to my team by doing it anyway. None of them ever physically attacked me, I was too big for most of them, it was always verbal's with Everton.

I even worked for some famous footballers, doing Steven Gerrards dad's party who were lovely polite people. Liverpool's x-manager Roy Evans was a great guy who I met while doing his brothers birthday party in some Chinese restaurant on the dockside. I even met Alan (Barney Rubble) Kennedy while DJ'ing after dinner speeches ironically underneath the very stands where we used to fight. So is life, and living in one city for fifty years throws these opportunities your way every now and again. Watching the reds in the city centre presents other opportunities; I got to speak to the great Ian Saint John, in the Rubber Soul pub in Mathew Street. He called me "big feller" because of my build and asked my opinion of the match verses Newcastle that we had just all watched. These moments come few and far between in your life and you must lap up every moment and remember what you did. The last brush with fame I had was in a very indirect way but it was the biggest one could ever have, as the wife's dad used to sail off to America in the early sixties. So, he used to bring rock and roll records home that the local kids couldn't get hold of. One of the lads from the music scene was a certain Paul McCartney, who he duly lent a few albums which he never actually got back. So indirectly Lynn's dad Harry could have radically changed the face of pop music in the UK. What a claim to fame that is.

Another claim to fame is being indirectly related by marriage to both Wayne Rooney and Tom Baker of Doctor Who fame, it really is a small world but there are a lot of famous people in this great city.

I personally find people of the current generation easily led by media commentators, back in the day it was you and your mates that formed independent opinions, which were not usually influenced by social media norms. In 2017 violence is not accepted anymore as it is not a socially accepted activity; however I suspect that it still exists down dark recesses of people's lives and in some less civilised countries of the world.

So, is hooliganism conquered? In some respects, it is because video evidence is blatant evidence to a committed act of violence. Joey Barton is another Huyton boy who got caught outside McDonalds in the city centre. But, violence is part of our survival instinct, and will carry on in one form or another as long as there is human contact and annoying bastards. The law is the rightful deterrent to violence, and I fought the law and the law won.

Here is a little bit of advice to all the younger generation who like to read about such things as what we did.

Life wastes away too fast if you let it so simply don't let it. Live for the day and do everything you want to (legally). You'll be 50 like me before you know it. So, live your life while you can and hopefully you'll have some great memories to look back on when you get old, and maybe enough memoirs to write a book about it. Never hold back because you worry about your facebook reputation or you perceived reputation, it's always a false profile anyway. If you live by too many rules your life will become boring. Go out, talk to people, mix and be alive. Don't watch TV magazine programs, and fill your time with pointless facts constantly thrown at you on normal TV. Don't watch any adverts, they are a waste of time.

It's full of 'fill your day' with dull information. Refine your knowledge by interest by watching personally filtered YouTube content that interest you instead. Always excel at everything you do. Be the best you can be. It's easier than you think, and I promise you will get results and become more fulfilled and a happier person, even if it offers scant financial reward.

Finally, always have a goal that excites you. Sorry for the rant, but I reckon that a few generations below me are losing focus as to what is important, to what is exciting and fun.

Here is a little extra bit of truth thrown at my by a good friend.
Jays story Watford away in 1983

Liverpool' next match was Watford. A group of us from Huyton made our way down to Lime Street station to the catch the football special. But when we arrived we got talking to a group of lads who said that all the boys were going on the ordinary train to Euston. So, we decided that we would join them. There was 120 on the ordinary. The train stopped at Stafford and another group of boys joined us. These lads followed Liverpool every week although they don't come from Liverpool, this made the crew about 135. The talk on the train was about if Watford had any boys as the year before there had been no trouble at all. We arrived at Euston at 11, and we all stuck together and made our way to the underground. We all jumped the barriers and made our way down the escalators without paying, this was the norm. We had to be alert as you can bump into other crews going to different grounds. Anyway, we made it to Watford without any trouble. When we all marched out the station we could see scouser's everywhere, the football special had arrived and the lads we knew told us they have got no boys. So, we all split up and went for a few pints then made our way into the ground and watched Liverpool win 2-0. At the end of the game all the boys joined together and made our way down to the town centre to catch the train, there must have been 1000 boys, you could feel there was something about to happen. Suddenly a lad produced a big metal rota blade and threw it through the jeweller's window, everybody rushed forward to grab the rings, the street was littered with jewellery and glass. Everybody was fighting to get a piece of jewellery and one lad managed to grab three pads and flagged a taxi and made off in another direction. Police sirens were going off everywhere and they were stopping people and searching them. A few people got arrested, a lot of people just shoved the jewellery down their undies or in their socks and headed straight for the train. This was just one of those days when there was no fighting yet it turned out to be a very profitable day for a lot of the boys. This happened on numerous occasions following Liverpool . Maybe we weren't the hardest mob in the country but we were game and by far the best at robbing and making money. This paid for future trips abroad. In the 80's we could pull a few hundred boys every week and we were the best dressed mob in the country, nobody can deny that.

Thanks to Merseyside Police for putting up with us.
Thanks to our mothers for putting up with us.
Thanks to Adidas for helping us run.
Thanks to all the glaziers that we helped live a profitable life.
Thanks to the general public for letting us have our fun in the eighties
and finally thanks to Liverpool FC for being the best and keeping us entertained in Europe, for a few hours.

My third book is out in October 2017, please follow my twitter account which is @oldcasuals2018. I have also written a sci-fi book, called Fallen angels.
My future plans are for an England hooligan book, maybe an 2018 hooligan book, as I think it seems to be all kicking off again and a book called Jack Thorn, which is a children's book about magic and all that stuff. (Harry Potter, Lord of the rings rip off)
Bye until the hooligans return and 'keep safe out there'.

29204652R00074

Printed in Great Britain
by Amazon